You Are
Unique

You Are Unique

Scale new heights
by Thoughts and Actions

A P J Abdul Kalam

Punya Publishing

First Published 2012 Reprinted 2012, 2013, 2014

PUNYA PUBLISHING PRIVATE LIMITED

Concept, editing

Dr Poonam S Kohli

Paintings

Neha Gouse

Cover

Shreevathsa Bhat

ISBN 81-89534-18-1

Published by

Sudhir for Punya Publishing Pvt. Ltd,

191, 16th Main, 24th Cross,

Banashankari 2nd Stage,

Bangalore - 560070

E-mail   info@punyapublishing.com

Website   www.punyapublishing.com

Contents

Unique You

The aim of one's life should be to reach one's full potential in body, mind, heart and spirit.

When we see the light of the electric bulbs, our thoughts go to the inventor Thomas Alva Edison for his unique contribution towards the invention of electric bulb and the electric lighting system. When we hear the sound of an aeroplane going over our house, we think of Wright Brothers, who proved at a heavy risk and cost to them, that man could fly. The telephone ring reminds us of Alexander Graham Bell. When everybody considered sea travel as an experience or a voyage, a unique person, during his sea travel from United Kingdom to India, was pondering why the horizon where the sky and sea meet looks blue? His research resulted in explaining the phenomena of scattering of light—this unique scientist Sir C V Raman was awarded Nobel Prize. The world is fortunate to have had a great leader of 20th century, Father of the Nation, Mahatma Gandhi, who got India its freedom, and also paved the way for South Africa's movement against apartheid. One woman scientist got two Nobel prizes; first in 1903 and the second in 1911. One was for discovering radium, and the other was for her pioneering research in chemistry. She is the discoverer of radiation that saved and is saving thousands and thousands of lives of cancer patients. And also now by irradiating the seeds certain types of agriculture crops are giving very high yields. The same radiation phenomenon is used both for power generation and also nuclear weapon system. Who is that great lady who made history in discovering radium that changed the nuclear material world and the healthcare world? The scientist is Madam Marie Curie. All these people and so many others like them HAVE WALKED INTO THE UNEXPLORED PATH AND STRIVED TO BE UNIQUE. THEY ARE REMEMBERED FOR THEIR CONTRIBUTION TO THE HUMAN KIND.

The question is: Are you willing to become a unique personality? I have, so far, met more than 11 million youth in India and abroad. I have learnt that, every youth wants to be unique, that is, YOU! But the world all around you, is doing its best, to make you just *everybody else*.

The challenge is to fight the hardest battle, which any human being can ever imagine; and never stop fighting until you arrive at your destined place, that is, a UNIQUE YOU! You have to decide, do you want to be a Unique You or Everybody else? If you have to be Unique You, you have to do, what Alexander Graham Bell suggested in 1905:

"Don't keep forever on the public road, going only where others have gone. Leave the beaten track occasionally and dive into the woods. You will be certain to find something you have never seen before. It will be a little thing, but do not ignore it. Follow it up, explore all around it; one discovery will lead to another, and before you know it, you will have something worth thinking about."

Alexander Graham Bell

The following poem inspired me during my school days.

Wings to Fly

You were born with potential.
You were born with goodness and trust.
You were born with ideas and dreams.
You were born with greatness.
You were born with wings.
You are not meant for crawling,

So I don't,
I have wings.
I will Learn to use them to fly.

- Jalaluddin Rumi
- 13th Century Persian Sufi Poet

The message is that education gives you wings to fly. Achievement comes out of the fire in our sub-conscious mind that "I will win." What is needed for realizing uniqueness is the culture of excellence and unique performance.

Culture of excellence

Excellence is not achieved by accident. It is a process, where an individual, (or an organization or nation,) continuously strives to better itself. For those who achieve excellence the performance standards are set by themselves, they work on their dreams with a focus and are prepared to take calculated risks and do not get deterred by failures as they move towards their dreams. Then they step up their dreams as they tend to reach the original targets. They strive to work to their potential, in the process, they increase their performance there by multiplying further their potential, and this is an unending life cycle phenomenon. They are not in competition with anyone else, but themselves. That is the culture of excellence. The culture of excellence needs an organization with youth with creativity, who strive to be unique.

Steps for achievement

How does one achieve what one wants? What will be your tools to fight this battle to be Unique? There are four tools for building a unique personality.
 • have an aim in life,
 • continuously acquire the knowledge,

- work hard and
- persevere to defeat the problems, succeed and realise the aim.

These are the four proven steps. If you acquire these four qualities, then you can achieve whatever you envision. Let me now share one poem, which I had written for the Parliamentarians, but which helps to imbibe the vision in one's life.

The Vision of the Youth

I climbed and climbed
Where is the peak of dreams, my Lord?
I ploughed and ploughed,
Where is the knowledge treasure, my Lord?
I sailed and sailed,
Where is the island of peace, my Lord?
Almighty, bless my nation
With vision and sweat resulting into happiness.

Once we have the Vision, what is needed to realize that vision is knowledge. Fundamental to becoming *a unique you*, is knowledge. The equation for knowledge is:

KNOWLEDGE = CREATIVITY + RIGHTEOUSNESS + COURAGE

Creativity

Inventions and discoveries have emanated from creative minds that have been constantly working and imagining the outcome in the mind. With imagining and constant effort, all the forces of the universe work for that inspired mind, thereby leading to inventions and discoveries.

Learning gives creativity,

Creativity leads to thinking,

Thinking provides knowledge,
Knowledge makes you great.

Righteousness

How do we inculcate the righteousness in the heart? In my opinion, there are three sources, which can build a personality with righteousness in the heart. One is mother, second is father, both in a spiritual environment, and the third and the most important is the teacher, particularly primary school teacher.

Courage

Another component in getting knowledge is courage. What kind of courage can be shown by the youth:

Courage to think different,

Courage to invent,

Courage to travel into an unexplored path,

Courage to discover the impossible,

Courage to combat the problems and succeed.

These are the unique qualities of the youth.

As a youth of my nation, I will work and work with courage to achieve success in all the missions.

The sources of knowledge are home, good books, teachers and teaching environment, coming into contact with good human beings, and teaching websites in the internet. When the schools will teach the students to use the knowledge with creativity, righteousness and courage, a nation will have a large number of empowered and enlightened citizens. Knowledge with creativity, righteousness and courage is vital for the growth of the individual, growth of the family, growth of the nation and promotion of peace in the world.

Building Confidence

The next important quality required in you is building confidence. Building confidence comes out of the company of great human beings.

They generate confidence in you by their life and teaching style. When I was studying in the fifth standard, many of us used to get less than 40 marks in mathematics. My mathematics teacher asked us when you are getting more than 80 marks in other subjects, why are you getting low marks in mathematics. Immediately, he evolved a method of teaching and creation of confidence for the whole class. How did the teacher inject the confidence in us? He conducted a class and gave us an exercise of 10 problems. In that exercise, more than 90% of the class including me got 100 out of 100. We were bubbling with happiness. Then onwards our mathematics performance improved. It was after many years we could realise that our teacher injected the confidence in us that *I can do it* by his teaching and also formulation of the problems to make us succeed and promote self-confidence. So to succeed in life, each one of you has to cultivate the confidence in you, that, "I can do". As a nation we should build the confidence, that "We can do".

Nothing Is Impossible

One of the main characteristics of the scientists is that they never say impossible, because what is impossible today, can become possible tomorrow.

Let not thy winged days, be spent in vain

As you all know, the earth rotates on its own axis once in a day having 24 hours or 1440 minutes or 86400 seconds. Earth itself orbits around the sun. It takes nearly one year for an orbit. With the completion of one rotation of earth around the sun, your age is added by one year as you are living on planet earth. Seconds fly, minutes fly, hours fly, days fly and years fly. We have no control over it. The only thing that we can do is, while the time flies, we can navigate the time. "Let not thy winged days, be spent in vain."

Save or better some one's life

The advice of Gandhiji's mother to her son was:

"Son, in your entire life time if you can save or better someone's life, your birth as a human being and your life is a success. You have the blessing of the Almighty God."

Every one of you should think how you can evolve yourself to save or better someone's life in your life time.

What I will be remembered for?

Finally I would like you to think, what would you like to be remembered for? You have to evolve yourself and shape your life. You should write it on a page. That page may be a very important page in the book of human history. And you will be remembered for creating that one page in the history of the nation—whether that page is the page of an invention, the page of innovation or the page of discovery or the page of creating societal change or a page of removing the poverty or the page of fighting injustice or planning and executing a mission of networking of rivers.

My best wishes to all of you in your endeavour to make a better nation and the world.

We will win, win, and win with our mighty will

When God is for me who can be against?

The poems in *You are Unique* might have also appeared in some of my other works but they are presented here in a unique way.

A P J Abdul Kalam

A Billion Smiles

Editor's Note

Dr A P J Abdul Kalam's two great human concerns have been how to bring smiles on the faces of billions of people and how to help people discover and retain their uniqueness.

For bringing smiles on the faces of people, he like an expert gardener observes with sympathy every pain of the society, every malady of the people and tries to cure it by working in weeding away its causes. His life and active concerns become a fountain of inspiration for so many others who help creating situations in reducing sorrows—physical, social, and emotional, of suffering humanity. Dr Kalam's mind can be best described in the words of William Blake:

On Another's Sorrow

Can I see another's woe,
And not be in sorrow too?
Can I see another's grief,
And not seek for kind relief?
Can I see a falling tear,
And not feel my sorrow's share?...

The most fascinating quality of Dr Kalam is his feeling the pain and sorrow of others and then making an untiring effort to mitigate it. The happiest moment of Dr Kalam's life was not when he received the highest honour as an Indian or highest position in the country but when he saw a polio struck child been able to run with a much lighter support for walking. For Dr Kalam the answer to a problem is, defeat the problem. If we are poor, should millions of our countrymen go without advanced health care heart stents? 'No', says Dr Kalam's indomitable spirit, and he looks for a solution in Kalam-Raju stent, which is much cheaper and within the reach of so many Indians.

Dr Kalam is a mystic as well as a scientist. He not only looks at the discoveries and inventions but also at the minds that worked on these inventions and encourages others to be like them. Follow an untrodden road fearlessly with indomitable courage is his clarion call to youth. It is easy to follow a beaten path; you remain in your comfort zone, so many may have already travelled by that path, the road is already made, you have only to walk on it. However, that will not help in bringing about any betterment or change in lives of people, which is the aspiration of Dr Kalam. He encourages one to discover one's *Unique You* and make a new road, face new difficulties, learn lessons from mistakes. This book *You are Unique* helps one to discover one's unique qualities, create a new road, tread a new path, see dreams, be passionate about them, work to mitigate the sorrows of others, create high-quality products, work with team spirit with a magnanimous heart and create high-quality institutions. Reflecting from his own life, he draws a road map for a great life, great leadership, and great institutions in this book.

Dr Kalam has a great faith in human potential and wants everyone to seek that uniqueness in oneself. The mystic in him takes over the scientist, and he encourages everyone to fight the hardest battle to retain one's uniqueness, discover and focus on one's core and work on what one can do best. The panacea of word's problems lies in that. Those who nurtured their unique self with courage have transformed the world.

You are Unique lays down the path and tells that the uniqueness for achievement needs to be supported with other human traits of righteousness, courage, vision, indomitable spirit, hard work, commitment, team spirit, magnanimity, truthfulness, and honesty.

The book makes a most enduring appeal for these aspects of personality that affects the intellect, the mind and which through its being an inherent truth gradually penetrate into the heart, producing the deep conviction and rational faith.

You are Unique is divided into four parts. It first convinces the reader about developing one's personality, and then shows the way of creative leadership to create great institutions with a sound value system, which will herald a brilliant future for all, described in Future Perspective.

Our ancient rishis, seers of truth, were alleviated above humanity and these truths were reflected by them in poetry. Music came out of their hearts. Same is true of Dr Kalam, his purest thoughts, in which he relates to the universe, effortlessly come out of him as poems. Poems that focus on the message of relating with other beings and giving, are artistically presented in the book as *Music From My Heart*.

No other modern teacher of life helps so much in developing one's inner self, core of ones being and righteousness as does Dr A P J Abdul Kalam in *You Are Unique*. His bright sun of intellectuality shines with sensitive heart that loves humanity. Intellectuality and heart, throbbing together, in prose and poems define a religion for tomorrow in *You Are Unique*.

This book is brought out in such a way as if Dr Kalam is talking to you answering your questions about life, work, management, and institutions. Holding your hand, it leads you without preaching, saying, this happened with me as well, and I did this, does it help you getting answers for your life and achieving success? He does not teach he lives his thoughts, and the intensity communicates and changes others. *You are Unique* thus; we hope, will help you discover your divinity and reflect it in every moment of life.

Poonam S Kohli

xvi

Rock Walls

Some build rock walls all their lives,
When they die miles of walls divide them.
Others build rock walls, one rock on another,
And then build a terrace, where they pray for love.

Yet others build walls to enclose orchards,
Endeavouring to find ways to fulfill hunger.
A few others build rock walls to make a home,
It is their mission to serve humanity and nature.

I build no walls, to confirm to joy or sorrow;
To sacrifice or achieve, or to gain or lose.
I just grow flowers on all open spaces,
And float lilies on ponds and rivers.

I keep planting trees, for birds to have nests,
At the dawn of the sun, when morning breeze
blows,
Sunlight gets filtered through shining tree
leaves,
Birds' flights give me sense of freedom and
pleasure.

Scattered lights of colour I treasure.
Fragrance of flowers gives me delight of creator.
Lotus floating over like nature's dance,
Why should I build walls to confine them all?
I have no house, only open spaces,
Filled with truth, kindness and dreams.
Desire to see my country developed and great,
And dreams to see everywhere happiness and peace.
Will you all work for converting this desire and dream into action?

Inner Motivation

Everyone has inside of him or her, a piece of good news.

The good news is, that you don't know how great you can be!

1

Preserve Your Divine Light

MY FATHER, JANAB AVUL PAKIR J AINULABDEEN, taught me a great lesson when I was a young school boy. It was just after India had won its independence. At that time panchayat board elections took place at Rameswaram. My father was elected a member of the panchayat board and on the same day he was also elected the President of the Rameswaram Panchayat Board. Rameswaram Island was a beautiful place with a population of 30,000. My father was elected President of the Panchayat Board not because he belonged to a particular religion or a particular caste or spoke a particular language or for his economic status. He was elected only because he had a noble mind and was a good human being. The following incident took place on the day he was elected President of the Panchayat board. I was studying my lesson. Those days we did not have electricity and we used to study under kerosene lamps, with kerosene bought in ration. I was reading the lesson loudly when I heard a knock at the door. In those days, we never used to lock the door of our house in Rameswaram. Somebody opened the door, came in and asked me where my father was. I told him that my father had gone for evening Namaz. Then he said, "I have brought something for him, can I keep it here?" Since my father was away for Namaz, I shouted for my mother to get her permission to receive the item. Since she was also on the Namaz there was no response. I asked the person to leave the item on the cot. After that I continued my studies.

I used to learn by reading aloud in my younger days. I was reading aloud and fully concentrating on my studies. My father came in and saw a *tambalum* kept on the cot.

He asked me, "What is this? Who has given that?"

"Somebody came and has kept this for you," I told him. He opened the cover of the *tambalum* and found a costly *dhoti*, an *angawastram*, some fruits and some sweets. He also saw the slip that the person had left behind. I was the youngest child, and my father loved me a lot. I also loved and respected my father a lot. He was upset at the sight of the *tambalum* and gifts left by someone. That was the first time I saw him very angry and it was also the first time I got a thorough beating from him. I got frightened and started weeping. My mother embraced and consoled me. Then my father came and touched my shoulder lovingly with affection and advised me not to receive any gift without his permission. He quoted an Islamic Hadith, which states that,

"When the almighty appoints a person to a position, He takes care of his provision. If a person takes anything beyond that, it is an illegal gain."

Then he told me that taking gifts like these was not a good habit. Gift is always accompanied by some purpose and so a gift is a dangerous thing. It is like touching a snake and getting the poison in turn. This lesson always stands out in my mind even when I am in my eighties.

The incident is deeply embedded in my mind. It taught me a very valuable lesson for my life. I would like also to mention the writing in *Manu Smriti*, which states that, *"By accepting gifts the divine light in the person gets extinguished."*

Manu warns every individual against accepting gifts for the reason that it places the acceptor under an obligation in favour of the person who has given the gift and ultimately this results in making a person do things not permitted by law.

I am sharing this thought with all of you, particularly the young people, do not be carried away by any gift which comes under the cover with a purpose and through which one may lose one's integrity.

- There is a difference between need and greed. When God gives a position to someone, he also takes care of his/her needs.
- Gifts bring expectation and obligation of favours.
- For staying upright and just, do not take gifts given with a purpose.

Question: You have been on such a high post, but how are you able to live such a simple life?

Answer: My needs are very few.

2

Righteousness

WHEN YOU HAVE A MISSION TO become a great corporate or entrepreneur, you need to possess two important qualities: RIGHTEOUSNESS IN LIFE AND INDOMITABLE SPIRIT.

Righteousness is imbibed in our culture and is part of our cultural strength. Righteousness gives us nobility. One of the greatest indicators of the nobility of the soul is to be JUST AND EVEN in the midst of trials and tribulations. Righteousness makes a man or woman carry on his/her business without any greed and without feeling proud of his ability to be of use to the society.

I am reminded of a Tamil classic, *Silapathikaram*, which brings out the power of righteousness and provides the code of conduct for the people in high and responsible positions.

It means that if people who are in high and responsible positions go against righteousness, the righteousness itself will get transformed into a destroyer. Whoever deviates from righteousness, whether it is the individual or the state, it is no more than a passing shadow. The errors of great men are like eclipses of the greater lights. Let this thought dwell in all of us and blossom into righteous actions, which are all the more important for those who deal with the affairs of the people. This message is brought out very clearly by Elangovadikal in *Silapathikaram*.

Silapathikaram is one of the five great epics written nearly 2000 years ago in Tamil language. The story of Kannagi plays an important role in the history of Madurai. Kovalan, a successful business man married Kannagi, who was the beautiful daughter of a merchant Maanaikkan. Later, Kovalan's life changed due to his association with the dancer Madhavi, and he lost all his property.

This led Kovalan to go back to his wife for help. Both went to Madurai to start trade after selling their only property, a pair of anklets called *Silambu*. In the meantime, the queen of Pandiyan King Nedunchezhiyan, lost her anklets (*Silambu*). Actually, the court jeweller had robbed the queen's anklets. Once the wicked jeweller happened to see Kovalan with Kannagi's anklets in the market. He seized the anklet from Kovalan and informed the King about it. The King sent guards to arrest Kovalan. Kovalan was accused of having stolen the queen's anklets and was killed as per the King's order.

When Kannagi came to know about the news she went out into the town, with her eyes ablaze with anger, carrying the other anklet in her hand as a proof of her husband's innocence. She made the King realise the truth by breaking her anklet, which was made of Manickam. When the Pandiyan King came to know that he had punished an innocent, he died in his throne saying, "Oh! I am the thief and he is not the thief." The queen also died at that spot. Kannagi burnt Madurai into ashes, in consequence to the injustice done to her husband.

Since the Pandiyan King had failed to preserve justice and punished an innocent person, righteousness transformed into a destroyer. This shows the importance of righteousness in our day to day life.

How to be righteous?

Listen To The Inner Voice For Being Righteous.

CONSCIENCE IS THE LIGHT OF THE SOUL THAT BURNS WITHIN THE CHAMBERS OF OUR PSYCHOLOGICAL HEART. IT IS AS REAL AS LIFE IS. IT RAISES THE VOICE IN PROTEST WHENEVER ANYTHING IS THOUGHT OF OR DONE CONTRARY TO RIGHTEOUSNESS. Conscience is a form of truth that has been transferred through our genetic stock in the form of the knowledge of our own acts and feelings as right or wrong.

A virtuous and courageous person alone can use the instrument of conscience. He or she alone can hear the inner voice of the soul clearly. In a wicked person this faculty is absent. The sensitive nature of conscience has been destroyed by sin or corruption in a wicked person. Hence, he or she is unable to discriminate right from wrong. **Leading organizations, business enterprises, institutions and governments should develop this virtue of the ability to use their own conscience. This wisdom of using the clean conscience will enable them to enjoy the freedom.**

Nobility of Mind

I had another unique experience many years back that reveals how a single leader can inspire a large population. I happened to meet, in Delhi, the granddaughter of Mahatma Gandhi, Mrs. Sumitra Kulkarni. She narrated to me an incident about her grandfather,

26

which she had personally witnessed. Mahatma Gandhi used to have a prayer meeting daily at a fixed time in the evening. After the prayers, there used to be a collection of voluntary gifts for the welfare of the under-privileged sections of society.

The devotees of Gandhiji used to collect whatever was given by the people and this collection was counted by the supporting staff of Gandhi family. Gandhiji was informed the details of the collections before his dinner and the next-day morning the money was handed over to a bank-man who visited them every morning. One day the bank man reported that there was a discrepancy of a few paise in the money given to him and the money collected. On hearing this, Mahatma Gandhiji went on fast saying that the contributions being collected is a donation for the poor and every paisa should be accounted for. Such was Gandhiji's integrity. His act of righteousness should be practised by all of us.

- Practise righteousness in all your thoughts and actions.
- Hear the voice of your conscience.
- Keep your mind clean.
- A virtuous person alone can hear the voice of his conscience.
- The voice of conscience discriminates between right and wrong.
- If we go against righteousness, the righteousness will turn into our destroyer.

3

Indomitable Spirit

IF YOU HAVE A MISSION TO BECOME a great leader, who can change the competitiveness index of an institution, I would like to share with you the need for possessing an important trait for success—indomitable spirit.

Let us study what constitutes the indomitable spirit. It has two components. The first component is that there must be a vision that would lead to higher goals of achievement. I would like to recall a couplet from Thirukkural, written 2500 years ago, by the Poet Saint Thiruvalluvar. It means that whatever may be the depth of the river or lake or pond, whatever may be the condition of the water, the lily flower always comes out and blossoms. Similarly, if there is a definite determination to achieve a goal, even if it is impossible to achieve, a man will always succeed.

Many of us have initiated and have also been a part of large programmes and projects. During the progress of these programmes, we would have many times experienced that success is not in sight and there are many hurdles. The same poet through another couplet, reminds us that we should never be defeated by any problems.

We should become the master of the situation and defeat the problems. I consider that these two Thirukkurals characterize the indomitable spirit. Such a spirit is crucial to improving the competitiveness of institutions, which can develop great human resources for adding value and generating wealth for the nation.

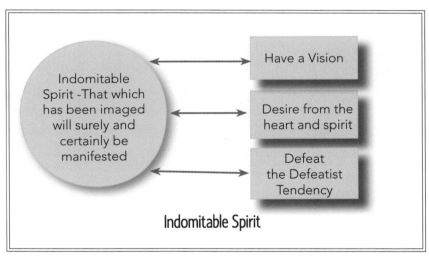

Indomitable Spirit

No night is without a dawn—Power of the mind

During my visit to Bulgaria, I was interacting with the students of Sofia University. One of the Indology students asked me, "I am a student practising Yoga. I read your book 'Wings of Fire'. I am keen to know from you about your experience with Swami Sivananda, which you have referred to in the book." I narrated the incident which took place way back in 1957. I had gone for my selection in the Indian Air Force to Dehradun and was ranked ninth in the selection results. But only eight candidates were commissioned. I knew that the days ahead would be difficult. I left Deharadun and reached Rishikesh on my way to Delhi. I took a bath in the holy river Ganga and walked to Sivananda Ashram, which is situated a little away up the hill. I met Swami Sivananda—a man who looked like Buddha. I was struck by his irresistible child-like smile and gracious manner. Before I could speak, he enquired about the cause of my sorrow. I told him about my unsuccessful attempt to join the Indian Air Force and my long-cherished desire to fly. His smile washed away all my anxiety, and he said:

"Desire, when it stems from the heart and spirit, when it is pure and intense, possesses an awesome electromagnetic energy. This energy is released into the ether each night, as the mind falls into the sleep state. Each morning it returns to the conscious state, reinforced with the cosmic currents. That which has been imaged will surely and certainly be manifested. You can rely young man, upon this ageless promise as surely as you can rely upon the eternally unbroken promise of sunrise. So, defeat the defeatist tendencies."

That was the unique interaction, I had with Swami Sivananda.

- Achieve a goal with will and determination.
- Defeat the defeatist tendency.
- Have an indomitable spirit.

Achieving Our Goals

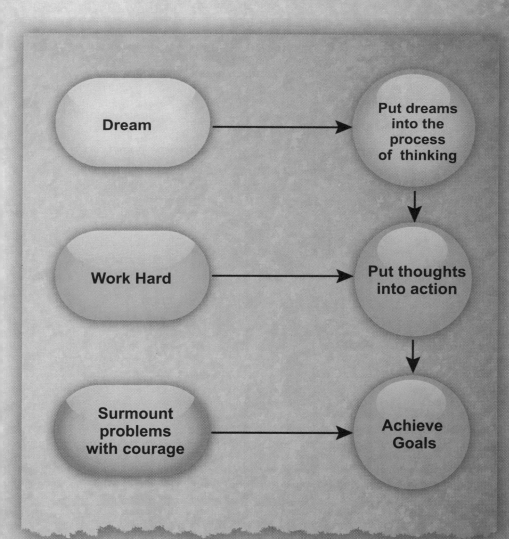

Indomitable Spirit

I was swimming in the sea,
Waves came one after the other
I was swimming and swimming to reach my destination.
But one wave, a powerful wave, overpowered me;
It took me along in its own direction,
I was pulled long and along.
When I was about to lose amidst the sea-wave power,
One thought flashed to me, yes, that is courage
Courage to reach my goal, courage to
defeat the powerful force and succeed;
With courage in my mind,
indomitable spirit engulfed me,
With indomitable spirit in mind and action,
I regained lost confidence
I can win, win and win
Strength came back to me, overpowered the sea-wave
I reached the destination, my mission.

(This poem was composed during a flight from New Delhi to Bangalore on 28th August 2010. The poem emanated as an answer to a number of questions posed to me from the youth on various issues and problems like, poverty, disorder in the family, invasion on Indian culture, mistrust, corruption, violence, terrorism and Maoism, distrust, underconfidence and fears that are prevailing among the youth. This poem is mainly to address the challenges, problems and fears encountered by the youth.)

4

Ignite a Vision

WITHOUT A VISION, WE CANNOT HOPE to look into the future. The first step to achieving a goal is to have a dream. Dreams turn into thoughts and thoughts generate action, and it is only concerted action that would result in achievement of our goals.

The Stories of Visions and Dreams

In the journey of life, very rarely some great human beings influence one's life. I had the privilege of working with three such personalities.

Space Visionary

I was fortunate to work with Prof. Vikram Sarabhai for seven years. While working closely with him, I saw the dawn of the vision for the space programme in a one-page statement. Witnessing the evolution and implementation of this one page by many years of ceaseless work by a cosmic-ray physicist and a great scientific mind, was really a great learning for me. Also I was thrilled to see the famous vision statement of Prof. Vikram Sarabhai, made in the year 1970, which states, "India with her mighty scientific knowledge and power-house of young, should build her own huge rocket systems (satellite launch vehicles) and also build her own communication, remote sensing and meteorological spacecraft and launch from her own soil to enrich the Indian life in satellite communication, remote sensing and meteorology." When I look at this vision statement in the present context, I am overwhelmed to see the results of this statement. Today, India can build any type of satellite launch vehicle, any type of spacecraft and can launch from Indian soil and also it has all the capability which its mighty great soul Prof. Vikram Sarabhai had imagined while starting his career in the laboratory of Sir C.V. Raman at the Indian Institute of Sciences.

Have you heard about Thumba? It is in Kerala on the seashore and is the place from where the Indian space programme commenced. There is an interesting story how Thumba was selected for the space program. Prof Vikram Sarabhai, a cosmic-ray scientist and Dr. Homi Bhabha a nuclear scientist were searching for a place from where they could launch sounding rockets for atmospheric research, ionospheric research and meteorological research. After seeing various places, they came to a conclusion that Thumba is the right place as it is very close to the Equator which will help the space research in equatorial zones.

NIKE CAJUN—a two staged rocket was launched in November 1963. That was an Indo-US APACHE cooperation Programme. Prof Vikram Sarabhai, within six years, unfurled the space mission for India that should build Satellite Launch Vehicle capability, to put India's communication satellite in the geosynchronous orbit and remote sensing satellite in the polar orbit. Also, he envisaged that launch vehicles built in India should be launched from Indian soil. This one visionary thought led to intensive research in multiple fields of science and space technology. Today, India with her thousands of scientific technological and support staff in multiple space research centres has the capability to build any type of satellite launch vehicles, any type of rockets and launch them from Indian soil. Sriharikota is the fortunate place in India from where all the space launches take place. I had the fortune to be part of Prof Vikram Sarabhai's vision and with my team participated in India's first satellite launch vehicle programme to put the satellite in the orbit.

Vision of Vivekananda

This thought came to me when I was in the beautiful environment of the renovated ancestral house of Swami Vivekananda in Kolkata. I recalled an event that took place in a ship which was sailing from Japan to Canada in 1893, when India was under British rule. Two great human beings were travelling in that ship. They were Swami Vivekananda and Jamsetji Nusserwanji Tata. They introduced each other and Swamiji asked Jamsetji Tata about where he was going and what was the mission of his visit. Jamsetji Tata said, "Swamiji, I am going with a mission to bring the steel industry to our country." It was year 1893, when India was ruled by the Britishers. Swamiji said, "It is indeed a beautiful mission. My best wishes. However, I would like to give you a small caution. Whatever amount you spend to get the process of making steel, simultaneously you should learn the metallurgical science of making steel also. I would prefer that you start an Institute, a laboratory to do advanced research on the subject." What a prophetic statement that came in the year 1893. Many things happened after that. Jamsetji Nusserwanji Tata could not get the technology for manufacturing steel from the UK. Jamsetji went to London and there he met the steel magnets and discussed about steel fabrication technology. He informed them that he had the resources to set up a fabrication facility. The British steel industrialists told Jamsetji, "If you Indians can make steel we Britishers will eat it."

But Jamsetji was not discouraged. He crossed the Atlantic and got the steel production technology from USA with all the blue prints and he prepared a road map and selected Jamshedpur as the place to locate the first steel plant. A large-scale planning took place. It had two parts: the first part was to start steel manufacturing plant at Jamshedpur, presently in Jharkhand. Simultaneously, he donated one-sixth of his property for establishing an Institute of Material Research at Bangalore.

He gave all the details to his successors and today the Tata Iron and Steel Company Jamshedpur produces nearly five million tonnes of steel. The Vision of Jamshetji Tata had two objectives—one to bring the technology, and another to make the country strong so that it could fight for its freedom. Jamsetji was responsible for putting the seedling for establishing the Indian Institute of Science for research in areas of material science. At Jamshedpur we can see the fruits of Jamsetji Nusserwanji Tata's vision: Tata Iron and Steel Company (TISCO). Due to his foresight, today India is self-reliant in steel technology. The other part of his vision, at Bangalore the seedling for the research laboratory has been transformed into a great learning centre—The Indian Institute of Science.

This incident demonstrates the vision of the great Swami Vivekananda. His vision was to have a strong and developed India. He clearly foresaw the role that science, technology and industry had to play for such a development. It was Swamiji who made Jagdish Chandra Bose to get a patent for his invention. Swamiji's call for awakening of India was not merely in spiritual fields but for all round economic and social progress.

The vision of J N Tata - Three missions

Jamsetji Nusserwanji Tata laid the foundation for three important projects. The first was the Tata Iron and Steel Plant, the second was the creation of hydro-electric power station, and the third was the establishment of an educational and research institute, popularly known as Tata Institute and now the Indian Institute of Science, Bangalore. Though Jamsetji Nusserwanji Tata envisioned all these institutions before his death in May 1904 but the Indian institute of Sciences—Bangalore opened its doors in 1911; the first ingot of steel rolled out from Tata Iron and Steel Plant in 1912; and the hydro-electric power was switched on in 1915 in Mumbai. Today, after 100 years of his demise we see all these three institutions flourishing and in full bloom. The Indian institute of Sciences Bangalore has become a world class institution. Tata Steel has crossed the five million tonnes per annum steel output. The Tata Hydro-Electric Station has been followed by many other power plants in the country. Tata's vision has brought a revolution in steel industry, power generation and education. I admire this great visionary, a visionary revolutionist who evolved a new method of working towards India's freedom through the development of industry, power and scientific research. The light he lit in our country has lit many lamps and is still lighting many more.

These are some of the examples that show how a vision gives a blue print for future development.

- Vision helps to look into the future.
- Without a vision we cannot plan for the future.
- Vision becomes a signpost for others and gives them direction and enthusiasm.
- The first step in achieving a goal is to have a dream.
- Dreams turn into thoughts and thoughts generate action.
- It is only concerted action which can result in achievement of our goals.

5

From Vision to Mission

Working in a Mission mode

DURING THE 1960S, INDIA WAS in a state of ship-to-mouth existence in food. If the American ships did not bring wheat, it would result in a famine in India. But there were two visionaries who worked together with the farming community and brought the first Green Revolution—the political thinker Shri C. Subramaniam and the agriculture scientist Dr. M.S. Swaminathan. Around the same time, Dr. Varghese Kurien masterminded the White Revolution. Today, we produce two hundred million tonnes of food grains, not only sufficient for us but most of the time available for export as well. Similarly, the white revolution resulted in placing India at the top of the world map of milk producers.

The need for a Mission and its role

In India, much innovation and creative thinking took place during the various phases of our development. Dr. Vikram Sarabhai said in the sixties that India should design and develop a large satellite launch vehicle and put communication satellite and remote-sensing satellite in geosynchronous orbit and polar orbit respectively. This vision statement ignited hundreds of scientists, technologists and thousands of technicians. Today, India is capable of building all types of satellite launch vehicles and satellites. Similarly, in missile area, we had a mission-oriented programme at DRDO that led to the deployment of two strategic missiles and the establishment of the capability to design, develop and produce any type of missiles.

Due to the vision of our nuclear programme, a series of nuclear power plants have been established adding 7000 megawatt power to our electrical grid of 100,000 megawatt. There is a proposal to increase the nuclear power to 20,000 megawatt by 2020.

In the year 1980, India had just started the work in the Information Technology. Some young entrepreneurs with their innovative and creative thoughts, within the difficult regime of our country's rules and regulations, demonstrated how IT enabled services can fetch export revenue. Subsequently, even the Government had to bring out innovative and liberalized IT policies. Now, our young IT entrepreneurs are generating export revenue of 50 billion dollars. This is expected to grow to more than 100 billion dollars by the year 2020. Similarly, the pharmaceutical industries are making a positive impact on the Indian economy. Our garment industry and our export of flowers and diamonds are not far behind. Our auto-component and automobile industries have made remarkable breakthroughs. Our cement industry has recorded great achievements in energy efficiency. Fly-ash utilization, which was just 3% in 1993, is now close to 25% after mission mode approach. It will further grow as fly-ash has multiple applications.

These successful missions give us the confidence that as a country we have the resources and the capability to succeed in challenging missions, if only we decide to achieve them. Our development should not be merely in the pattern of 'following the West' like the US, Europe or Russia, we have to ensure that we achieve the development goals keeping our civilization's heritage intact. Then alone will prosperity and peace blend together. We must ensure that the development brings harmony at home, order in the nation and peace in the world. For that righteousness is the basic requirement, which is to be promoted among all citizens of the country.

A coherent vision owned by every one turns to a common mission.

During one of my visits to Dubai, I met the ruler of Dubai. He said that Dubai is planning to increase its tourist arrival by five times. Once this decision was taken, I found a coherent plan of work started getting implemented. The aviation minister was planning for a new airport and purchases of new types of aircraft needed for attracting the tourists. The surface transport minister was planning a number of additional lanes required in the highways. The works' ministry was planning for an increase in the hotel accommodation for the tourists. The health ministry had a road map for the waste management and additional clean water requirements. This was the type of integrated response of the whole government to fulfil the national objective. A leader should appreciate the message out of this experience. For any successful mission, we should plan to work together with foresight in a mission mode for the multiple requirements of development of any kind.

Coherent Vision to Missions

Aim great missions, work for them and you will achieve your goals.

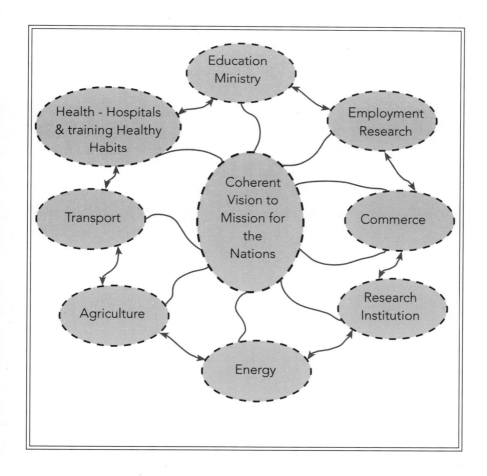

Transforming an island into a missile launch complex

I was working for India's missile programme from 1982 to 1999. Even though my place of work was Hyderabad, my theatre of action was always Chandipur and Wheeler Islands of Orissa coast where the developed missiles were flight-tested. I would like to narrate an interesting experience which happened during that period.

In October 1993, the development of Prithvi missile was almost over. However, the Army desired to have a confirmatory test, on a land range, to validate the Circular Error Probability (CEP) of the missile. Our efforts to conduct the tests in our desert range could not take - off due to the range safety problems. To overcome this, we were looking for an uninhabited island in the Eastern coast. On the hydrographic map supplied by the Navy, we saw a few islands in the Bay of Bengal off Dhamra (Orissa coast) indicating that there was some landmass. Our range team consisting of Dr. S.K.Salwan and Shri V.K. Saraswat hired a boat from Dhamra and went in search of the island. On the map, these islands were marked as Long Wheeler, Coconut Wheeler and Small Wheeler. The team carried a directional compass and proceeded on the journey. They lost their way and could not locate the Wheeler Island. Fortunately, they met few fishing boats and asked them for the route. The fishermen did not know about the Wheeler Island, but they said there was an island called Chandrachood. They thought that this could be the Wheeler Island. They gave the approximate direction for proceeding to Chandrachood. With this help, the team could reach the Chandrachood Island, which was later confirmed as the Small Wheeler Island. By this time, it was late in the evening and was dark.

The boatman refused to move in the night, and the team had to stay in the Small Wheeler Island in the boat for the night counting the stars. The next morning the team returned to Dhamra. On the physical survey of the three islands, it was found that the Long Wheeler Island had eroded over a period of time and was not useful for range activities. In view of this we chose the Small Wheeler Island, which had adequate width and length required for range operations. The team also found some signs of boats from other countries visiting the Small Wheeler Island. A study of the hydrographic data of a number of years indicated the erosion characteristic of the island. After taking over the islands from the Orissa Government for range activities, we created permanent stony bunds on the periphery of the selected islands to prevent any future erosion. This one tiny island has since been transformed into a world-class missile range complex in a very short period. What we learn from this experience is: aim for a great mission, work for it and you will succeed.

- Vision should translate into mission leading to organizational goals.

- Mission creates an energy in the organization to achieve goals.

- Aim for a great mission, work for it and you will succeed.

- Success of a mission is possible when everyone owns it and works in a coherent manner to achieve it.

- Developmental goals should keep our civilizational heritage intact.

Awake, arise and stop not till the goal is achieved.

Swami Vivekananda

Question: What is India's biggest obstacle
to becoming a developed nation?

Answer: Self-doubt.

6

Removal of Self-doubt

One of the Keys For the Progress of Human Beings

DR. STEPHEN HAWKING OF Cambridge Uuniversity is one of the
most accomplished physicists of our time. This great scholar was affected
by a motor neuron disease which deteriorated so much that it threatened his
research career. His speech became slurry and many people predicted
that he would not live to complete his Ph.D. His determination and
the help that he received from modern technology as well as from some
close friends made sure that he not only lived to complete his Ph.D., but
also made the most enviable contribution to Physics—the string theory.
He is a great living example that glorifies the confidence to win despite
a number of physical disabilities.

During my visit to Bulgaria in 2003, I visited the National Art
Gallery of Bulgaria. There I saw an exhibition of paintings, mostly

46

done by Bulgarian painters which inspired and impressed me. I also saw the 100th birth anniversary exposition of the famous Bulgarian artist Zlatju Bojadjiev. Hundreds of paintings were done by him using his right hand, as is normally done. I was told that his right hand was subsequently paralyzed. But the indomitable spirit in him, made him paint using his left hand and these more beautiful paintings which were also displayed were painted with his left hand. What struck me was that CONSTRUCTIVE PEOPLE CANNOT BE HAMPERED BY A PHYSICAL DEFECT, AS THE POWER COMES FROM WITH IN TO MAKE ONE GO AHEAD WITH THE LIFE'S MISSION.

Nani Palkhivala started his life as a middle class boy who suffered from stammering but his father, noticing his clear thinking and incredible debating power, repeatedly advised him to take up the legal profession. Nani aspired for the ICS, but fate destined otherwise. What a great boon to the nation it was to have had the spectacle of Palkhivala, in his lawyer's robes appearing before the Supreme Court and the judges remarking, "Such arguments will not be heard in this Court for centuries."

Sir C V Raman was head of teaching and research in Physics and created great scientific leaders and was also instrumental in the inception of Raman Research Institute, Bangalore. At the age of 82, Sir C V Raman, while addressing young graduates said:

"I would like to tell the young men and women before me not to lose hope and courage. Success can only come to you by courageous devotion to the task lying in front of you. I can assert without fear of contradiction that the quality of the Indian mind is equal to the quality of any Teutonic, Nordic or Anglo-Saxon mind. What we lack is perhaps courage, what we lack is perhaps the driving force which takes one anywhere. We have, I think, developed an inferiority complex. I think what is needed in India today is the destruction of that defeatist spirit.

47

We need a spirit of victory, a spirit that will carry us to our rightful place under the sun, a spirit which will recognise that we, as inheritors of a proud civilization, are entitled to a rightful place on this planet. If that indomitable spirit were to arise, nothing can hold us from achieving our rightful destiny."

These were the words from the Nobel laureate scientist of India that always reverberate in my mind.

- Self-doubt is the biggest hurdle in your way to progress.
- Productive people cannot be hampered even by physical defects.

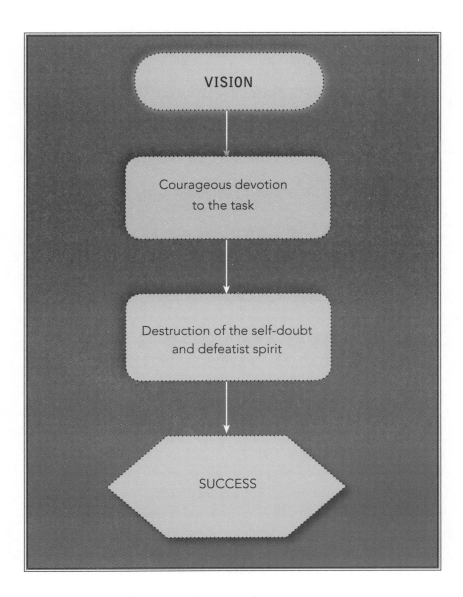

The path to achieve Success

Question : What is the secret of your success —your self-confidence or your efforts or your determination?

Answer : Sweat, Sweat and Sweat. When you work you will definitely come across some problems. Do not allow problems to become your master. You become the master of the problems and succeed.

7

The love for one's work

SRINIVASA RAMANUJAN LIVED ONLY FOR 33 YEARS and did not have a formal higher education or a means of living. Nevertheless, his inexhaustible spirit and love for his subject made him contribute to the treasure house of mathematical research— some of which is still under serious study and has been engaging the efforts of mathematicians all over the world to establish formal proofs. Ramanujan was a unique Indian genius who could melt the heart of the most hardened and outstanding Cambridge mathematician Prof G H Hardy. In fact, it would not be an exaggeration to say that it was Prof. Hardy who discovered Ramanujan for the world. Professor Hardy rated various geniuses on a scale of 100. While most of the mathematicians got a rating of around 30 with rare exceptions reaching to 60, Ramanujan got a rating of 100. There cannot be any better tribute to either Ramanujan or to Indian heritage. His works cover vast areas, including Prime Numbers, Hyper-geometric Series, Modular Functions, Elliptic Functions, Mock Theta Functions, even magic squares, apart from serious side works on geometry of ellipses, squaring the circle, etc. One of the tributes to Ramanujan says that, 'every integer is a personal friend of Ramanujan'.

Number theory and spiritual connectivity

Ramanujan used to say "An equation means nothing to me, unless it expresses a thought of God." For him, the understanding of numbers was a process of spiritual revelation and connection. In his investigations into pure mathematics, he drew extraordinary conclusions that mystified his colleagues, but were eventually, usually proven to be right. He opened a universe of theory that until today is reaping applications. The landscape of the infinite was to Ramanujan a reality of both mathematics and spirit.

He would talk for hours on the relationship he saw between God, zero and infinity. He spoke of the quantity 2 to the power 'n' minus one ("2n-1"), explaining that it stood for "the primordial God and several divinities. When n is zero, the expression denotes zero, there is nothing; when n is "1," the expression denotes God; when n is "2," the expression denotes Trinity; when n is "3," when n is "7," the expression denotes the "*Saptha Rishis*" (a group of seven stars called the "Great Bear"). And he continued with the idea that "Zero represents Absolute Reality. Infinity is the myriad manifestations of that Reality. Their mathematical product, Infinity x 0 is not one number, but all numbers each of which corresponds to individual acts of creation." For Ramanujan, numbers and their mathematical relationship were the measure of how the universe fits together. Each new theorem he explored was one more piece of the infinite to fathom.

51

Communication models

One of the important applications of the Number Theory is in designing error correcting codes which are robust against noise introduced in communication channels. The idealistic communication models can be described as follows:

Source to Encoder to Channel (added with noise) to Decoder to Receiver.

Working for the beauty and purity of work– Not for immediate gains

The problems of defining a suitable measure of information and of efficiency of coding have been satisfactorily solved. The second problem of coding is concerned with finding a method whereby for each message received, we can identify the message transmitted with the least amount of error, even when the transmitted message is corrupted by noise. The fundamental theorem of information theory assures us that under certain conditions this can be done. The construction of error correcting code has been a difficult and fascinating mathematical problem, and its more or less successful solution has made it possible for us to think of channels or great reliability to work with computers and automation equipment.

In the area of analogue signal processing a mathematical technique called Fourier Transform is used. When one enters the digital world a different tool called the Discrete Fourier Transform is used. Whereas, if one has to analyse noise signals, engineers have recently come to the conclusion, that an efficient mathematical tool would be the Ramanujan Fourier Transformation or in short RFT. This once again demonstrates that though RAMANUJAN DID THE WORK ON RFT PURELY TO SATISFY HIS URGE TO EXPLORE THE BEAUTY OF MATHEMATICS, IT HAS COME TO BE OF USE IN DAY-TO-DAY APPLICATIONS LIKE COMMUNICATIONS— ALMOST SIX DECADES LATER.

Cryptography and Information Security

Number Theory once epitomized pure mathematics. Today, the applied Number Theory usually refers to Cryptography, which enables secure communications. Very simple mathematics, used cleverly, occasionally produces spectacular practical results. Indeed the first public key crypto systems needed only the most rudimentary number theory. But the modern elaborations of the number theory use all the number theoretic tools one can reasonably expect from an undergraduate. Thus, cryptography motivates a new generation of students to study the number theory. Cryptography aside, applied number theory might also mean communication networks. Expander graphs are basic building blocks in the design of networks and have vast number of applications in areas of computer and communication sciences. In the last two decades the theory of Ramanujan Graphs has gained prominence primarily for two reasons. First, from a practical point of view these graphs resolved an external problem in communication network theory. Second, from a more aesthetic point of view.

In the digital world, bits and bytes represent knowledge which in turn represents the nation's wealth. For example, the source codes of the software that a company sells, the long term strategies of companies, bank accounts, the purchase through e-commerce and even our land records are in digital form today. Movement of bits across the network creates further wealth in the digital era. More than 25% of most nations soon will be directly or indirectly connected with Information and Communication products. In this new world, the economic and physical securities are closely intertwined by information security. Nations that are capable of generating and managing information in a secure way will become world leaders and world super powers.

Cryptography—the art of hiding information is central to information security. There are two major ways by which information can be cryptographically secured in computer mediated communication.

One is the symmetric cipher where the same key is used for encryption as well as decryption. The other is the Asymmetric key cryptography, wherein the encryption key and the decryption key are different.

The latter can be also used for Public-Key Encryption. The Asymmetric key cryptography like the widely used RSA (Ron Rivest, Adi Shamir and Len Adleman) is dependent on the complexity of calculations needed for finding out the two prime numbers p and q, given their product $n = p \times q$. This is where Number Theory comes in—a field wherein Ramanujan made long lasting contributions. Had Ramanujan lived for a few more years, had we continued to maintain the lead that Ramanujan gave us in the field of Number Theory; today we would have become the "Leaders in Secure communication" and possibly made many innovations that would have made our nation proud and also rich. Ramanujan, in making contributions to Number Theory was well ahead of his time—blissfully unaware of the potential of his work either in securing information or in creating wealth. HE DID WHAT HE DID SIMPLY FOR THE BEAUTY AND PURITY OF IT. What Ramanujan said is so much, what he implied is even more, and what he left behind is the legacy that many generations would never forget and perpetuate his mission.

Information & Communication Technology (ICT)

ICT has established that the data transformed into information has a business proposition which has given a competitive advantage. I am sure that by the end of this decade countries like India will have IT enabled services in the fields of human resources, customer interaction, finance and accounting, data search and integration, e-education, tele-medicine and e-governance.

Core competencies that can be exploited in addition to the above include information security, scientific software development that can spearhead a strong domestic market, entertainment, education, hardware and chip design and wireless. In India the software industry is exploring these areas to create a wealth of $80 billion in a few years. We strongly believe that with a proper planning and the ability to move up the value chain we may even touch a target of $150 billion in a decade.

- Work done with passion and sincerity has its own reward.
- The contribution of such work may not be measurable immediately but its fragrance may inspire generations to come.
- Institutions are made by the sincere work of individuals who work for the love of it.
- Let history judge the value of footprints of your work that you leave on the sand of time.

..... And what is it to work with love?
It is to weave the cloth with threads drawn from
your heart, even as if your beloved were to wear
    that cloth.
.....It is to charge all things you fashion with a breath
    of your own spirit...
Work is love made visible.

Kahlil Gibran

Question : What can we do to be someone like you?

Answer : When you are young, you need to have an ambition for life. Think big and continuously acquire knowledge. Once you know what you would like to become, you have to sweat for it. That means hard work. While you are progressing, there will be problems and hurdles. You must have an indomitable spirit and perseverance to defeat the problems. Then you will succeed in life. Remember that the Almighty is with you, and he will collude for your success.

8

Nurture
the Unique You
National Mission For Nurturing Mathematicians

WHEN WE ALL TALK ABOUT THE nation's strides in IT, space, defense, agriculture and academic institutions we have not yet fully recognised the importance of mathematics. It is becoming more and more difficult to get bright young students taking Mathematics—the purest of the sciences—as a career. This dearth of students will in the next few years stifle innovations. There is a need to launch a national mission to generate mathematicians in large numbers and also create suitable employment potential for them, so that we may be able to enrich our scientific work and our national tradition of mathematics that goes back to thousands of years. This is eminently possible since India for several centuries had been the home of some of the best talents in mathematics—a tradition that should be nurtured for the world to benefit.

58

There may be hundreds of minds spread over the country with mathematical bent of mind. They are looking for the gifted senior scientists and professors to encourage their thinking to make the best contribution in the field. We have to shed the 'minimum educational qualification syndrome for the sake of discovering and encouraging the dreams of the young minds. Throughout the country, the educated community, blessed with higher educational potential, should spot and encourage the creative minds, wherever they are, irrespective of their regions.

Early recognition of talents

The genius in Ramanujan had to be discovered by Prof. Hardy. Commenting on the fact Poondi Namasivaya Mudaliar had said with anguish, "It is the destiny of our nation that an Indian brain requires an acknowledgement from a foreigner. Why are our people hesitant to appreciate such a personality?"

I would like to narrate another incident which took place a few years back. A young man, Loveligen, from a remote area of Kerala, who could not complete PUC, wrote to me saying that he had discovered a new mathematical theory and that he would like to talk to me. I could sense from the letter that the boy was very sincere. I thought our specialist team could study his work and direct him to the right type of researchers. I called this boy to Delhi for a few days. What surprised us was that he had arrived at part of the equations of the Ramanujan's number theory, which this boy was not at all aware. He had discovered something and added some new points to it and the result was new.

To a great extent, the achievements in the field of mathematics seem to come out of a desire to look into the beautiful aspects of nature, including natural phenomena such as the star-studded skies, which have interested the astronomers from time immemorial. An additional contributory factor seems to be an inherent drive towards recognition of patterns, even if it be in the sense of mathematical sequences or series.

It is interesting to note that Loveligen has currently delved into the equally exciting topic of power sequences and series. What I felt was that he needed a good mathematical education or a patronage of a good mathematics teacher. It is like having Prof Hardy for Ramanujan, for the mathematics genius to flower. I asked this boy, why he hadn't met a mathematics teacher. He said, meeting a mathematics teacher was an expedition. Most of the teachers felt it below their dignity to meet somebody who was not even a graduate.

How do we promote these kinds of young and enthusiastic minds? Can our teachers and philanthropists or the social activists spot these buds and help them to blossom? Those who spot such talents and make them blossom will themselves be a different kind of a flower, as described in the Bhagwad Gita:

"See the flower, how generously it distributes its perfume and its honey. It gives to all, gives freely of its love. When its work is done, it falls away quietly. Try to be like the flower unassuming despite all its qualities."

What a beautiful message for all generations of this nation.

I have asked Dr. R. Chidambaram, Dr. R. A. Mashelkar and Prof. N Balakrishnan, great scientists and teachers, to evolve a system to provide an outlet for innovativeness in the budding mathematicians. One of the suggestions that I have is that, to nurture Indian talents, like the way Hardy did for Ramanujan, many of the mathematicians must agree to host these talents at least for a few months in their institutions. People like the ones mentioned earlier could become great teachers of tomorrow, by helping to shape the uncut diamonds to polished jewels that we could be proud of. We should create more Ramanujan in the field of mathematical sciences. For this, we also need persons with the mind like Prof Hardy to spot geniuses and nurture them in all walks of their lives.

Capacity building model

When students come out of the University, certain capacities, are required to be built in them for enabling them to face the challenges of the real world, in their professional career and also to facilitate their participation in the task of national development. I suggest that the ingredients for capacity building must be embedded right from the beginning of the student life. A good educational model is the need of the hour to ensure that the students grow to contribute towards the economic growth of a nation.

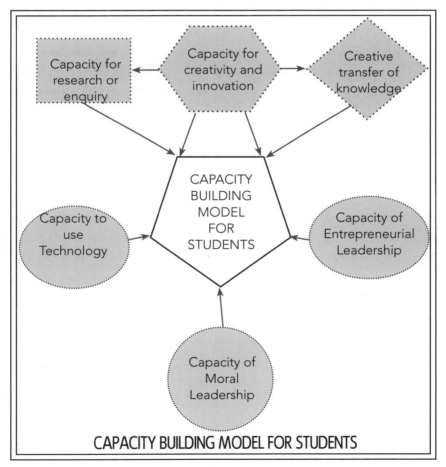

CAPACITY BUILDING MODEL FOR STUDENTS

For participating in the nation building tasks, the following capacities are required to be developed among the students in their formative years by the educational institutions:
- ✦ the capacity for research or inquiry,
- ✦ the capacity for Creativity and Innovation, particularly the creative transfer of knowledge,
- ✦ the capacity to use technology,
- ✦ the capacity for entrepreneurial leadership and
- ✦ the capacity for moral leadership.
- ✦ Research and enquiry

THE 21ST CENTURY IS ABOUT THE MANAGEMENT OF ALL THE KNOWLEDGE AND INFORMATION WE HAVE GENERATED AND THE VALUE ADDITION WE BRING TO IT. We must give our students the skills of life-long learning with which they can find a way through the sea of knowledge that has been and being created. Today, the technology has enabled us to teach ourselves to become the life-long learners. This is required for sustained economic development.

As an example, I would like to share with you the discussion I had with one of my friends on how to activate both sides of the brain in a balanced way, so that the child can have concentration and high-efficiency learning. We discussed the use of abacus in developing the capability of the child. Immediately, I searched for the information on the abacus and its tools on the internet. I found a number of sites that provide simulated training through computers and animated packages for self-learning as well as various other related tools in the form of mathematics games which make the learning process a beautiful experience.

The faculty members should inculcate this capacity of inquiry among the students, and the universities should provide the environment and infrastructure for the students to learn by themselves with the help of live examples.

IN SUM, INQUIRY, CREATIVITY, TECHNOLOGY, ENTREPRENEURIAL AND MORAL LEADERSHIP ARE THE FIVE CAPACITIES REQUIRED TO BE BUILT THROUGH THE EDUCATION PROCESS. IF WE DEVELOP IN ALL OUR STUDENTS THESE FIVE CAPACITIES, WE WILL PRODUCE "AUTONOMOUS LEARNERS" SELF-DIRECTED, SELF-CONTROLLED, LIFE-LONG LEARNERS WHO WILL HAVE THE CAPACITY OF BOTH, TO RESPECT AS WELL AS QUESTION THE AUTHORITY, IN AN APPROPRIATE MANNER. These are the leaders who would work together as a "self-organizing network" and transform any nation into a developed nation in a time-bound manner.

Employment Generation through Entrepreneurship

There has been a substantial growth in our higher educational system all over the country. Around three million students graduate per annum from 300 universities. However, our employment generation system is not in a position to absorb the graduates passing out from the universities leading to an increase in the educated unemployed in the region year after year. There is a large mismatch between the skills required for the modern economy, and the education imparted to most of these students. In addition, economic growth and investments have not kept pace with the availability of human resources. This situation will lead to instability in the social structure. We need higher education that focuses on and is oriented towards high value and productive employment opportunities. A three-pronged strategy is needed that makes education more attractive, imparts skills and generates employment potential in an individual. How do we do that?

Firstly, the educational system should highlight the IMPORTANCE OF ENTREPRENEURSHIP and students during the college education should be oriented towards setting up of the enterprises which will provide them creativity, freedom and ability to generate wealth. It should be taught to all the students, that **diversity of skills and perseverance in work makes an entrepreneur.** In addition, college syllabi for arts, science, and commerce courses should include topics and practicals for entrepreneurship training.

Secondly, the banking system should provide venture capital, from the village level to the prospective entrepreneurs for undertaking new enterprises.

Thirdly, there has to be an economic pull for human resources; for example, the generation of marketable products and enhancement of purchasing power among the people through the implementation of national missions.

The educational institutions, government and the private enterprises should become facilitators for creating entrepreneurship schemes through the support of the banking system and the marketing system. Entrepreneurs have to produce competitive products for becoming successful in their missions. I am sure that in this way the capacities of many graduates, will be built for becoming entrepreneurs and being employers rather than the employees.

- Nurture talents and create new leadership in every field.
- Be a mentor providing an encouraging environment for inherent genius and capacities to flower.
- Inquiry, creativity, technology, entrepreneurial and moral leadership are the five capacities required to be built through the education process.
- Diversity in skills and perseverance in work make an entrepreneur.

MUSIC FROM THE HEART

Music is born out of poems
Poems are born out of thoughts
Thoughts spring from creative minds.

I would like to share one event which took place on the last evening, 24th July 2007 of my tenure at Rashtrapati Bhavan, which is the house of the President of India. I went around all the gardens. Certain beautiful events occurred during the visit and also unique scenes flashed through my mind. I composed the poem in an integrated way depicting all that I saw and imagined. The name of the poem — ***What Can I give.***

What can I give

1.

One evening, a beautiful evening
I was in a mission of thanks giving
To my families of nature.
Reached the hut in the Mughal Garden
In the midst of dense banyan grove.
Herbal fragrance filled all around,
Musical fountain with rhythm of Shehnai.

Hundreds of intoxicated parrots by the music.
One young banyan tree, talked to me "O! Kalam
In all seasons, with trunks rooted on earth
We absorb all the heat in the mid days
We give shelter to so many birds.
Give shade and cool breeze
To animals and humans all around.
What man gives, tell me Kalam."

"O my young friend, you have given
    A great message of Giving,
Continue your God's mission of giving and giving."

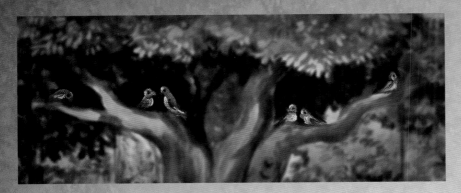

2.
Suddenly many parrots came and sat
All around the branches of the trees
In the serene banyan grove,
Lighted the place beautiful and glittering.
One Parrot, shot a question to me,
"We the parrots are beautiful!
As your poetic words picture us
O Kalam, can you fly on your own?"
   "O! No my friends, you are blessed,
     Continue the mission of spreading happiness."
     My human pride completely melted.

3.
A new scene emerged
With a family of eight peacocks and peahens,
Surrounding me seated in the hut
Three of the peacocks with fully unfurled wings,
Danced and danced, it was a heavenly sight,
Never seen, three peacocks in my garden,
All dancing in a place same time,
Time stood still.
A younger one looked at me
   "Kalam sir, can you remember me?"
   "O friend, you are all alike."
The peacock said, I was the one lying semiconscious
In front of your office, you brought the doctor, Sudhir

You touched me with kindness.
Then I did not know anything,
Except I was on the operation table of Sudhir.
The tumor in my throat was removed,
Medicine given and I was fed and cured.
The doctor handed over me to you,
You blessed me and let me fly.
In Biodiversity park with happiness rising
Today Kalam sir, we gave you
A final thanks giving dance."
    "O my young friend,
      God has blessed you with
      A great quality called gratitude
      Continue spreading it wherever you go!"

4.
Entered into the bio-diversity park
Deer herds with their little ones
They ran and ran,
The leader marching with horns straight,
Glanced at me and said "I am the leader of the deer."
There was a formation of deer,
The horned leader was bowing his head
Then a miracle happened.
One lovely deer, a young one slowly and
Slowly advanced towards me,
And started licking my hand
Looked at me and said "I am the little one
You daily fed me with milk,

When my mother had forsaken me,
As I could not walk or run to reach her.
Thank you sir, feeding me milk
many a days,
And for curing my injuries.
You and Sudhir gave life to me."
  This event electrified me,
    Bowing their heads with tears rolling
    From the return of Kindness.
    The deer herd slowly advanced.

5.

The sun was setting.
Full moon was rising from the horizon
Spiritual garden was welcoming,
"O' Kalam we have a message for you
We are a family of dates, olive, tulsi trees.
And many more,
look at us,
We grow together
We live together,
 Muslims, Christians, and Hindus,
And those from other religions
Adore us,
individually.
Breeze embraces all of us,
In all seasons,
We give freshness and fragrance,
Kalam, you can tell about us,
To all your citizens."

"O! My spiritual gurus,
You are indeed giving a great message on Unity of Minds."
That was indeed for me a treat, from the university of learning.
 I got answer, what can I give.

6.
The nature's citizens inspired.
What can I give?
Yes, removing the sorrow of the needy,
Gladdening of the sad heart,
And above all, I realized in giving,
Happiness radiates all around.

(Composed at the Mughal Garden on 24th July 2007.)

The Great Tree In My Home

Oh the tree* in my home,
You are great, among trees,
So many generations were enriched
Through decades, with your help, so kind,
Many now live under your sagely care,
Your song of life, I love to hear.

Oh my friend Kalam,
I crossed age hundred like your father and mother.
Everyday morning, you walk an hour
I also see you on full moon nights,
Walking with a thinking mood.
I know my friend, the thoughts in your mind,
"What can I give?"

When in April, you look at me,
Again and again with deep concern,
Seeing me shed thousands of leaves,
You ask me my friend, What is my burden?
Leaves I shed to give birth to new leaves,
Flowers bloom attracting butterflies and bees.
So, Kalam, it is not burden for me,
It is a beautiful phase of my life.
Year after year, says the tree,
"I give and give."
So I remain young and happy.

Now Kalam, take a tour with me,
See closely inside, in my dense branches,
A large beehive full of honey,
Built by thousands of worker bees,
Honey collected by their ceaseless work.
Honey-hive so heavy, with sweet honey drops,
Guarded well by thousands of bees.
For whom, this honey is collected and guarded,
It is for you all, rich and poor,
Our mission is to give to every life.

Oh Kalam, did you see so many nests,
Built by various birds in my branches.
Most of the top branches of my tree attract,
Hundreds of parrots as their home.
You have rightly called me parrots' tree.
Nowadays, you call me also honey tree,
When I hear you talking to your grandson about me,
I smile and smile.
I give many homes to birds in my branches and trunk holes.
I have heard songs of birds, and seen, love, birth and growth.
The birds are flying and flying around me sharing happiness.
And also, sometimes, with fear of eagles.

Nowadays, Kalam, daily during your walk,
You come close to me to see my root,
All-around dense flower garden with a velvet grass bed.
To a peahen,
The peahen giving warmth to the eggs.
All the time giving safe breeding with motherly love.
It is a beautiful sight in your home.
The peahen with its seven kids,
Majestically walking all around me,
And guarding the children day and night.

Now, you question Kalam, what is my mission?
Mission of hundred years of my life.
My mission, I enjoy giving what all I have,
I share—flower and honey, give abode, to hundreds of
birds.
I give and give.
So, I remain always, young and happy.

*The Indian name of the tree–Arjuna, Botanical name– Terminalia.
(The poem was presented at the Poet's Meet at Queen's University
Belfast, Northern Ireland on 10th June 2009.)

Radiating message from Sree Siddaganga Math

You, in front of you, see a sage.
Wearing beautiful spiritual blessings, the sage,
Everyday, Almighty has given this sage,
A precious diamond of life.
The sage, strung over thirty six thousand,
Diamonds into a priceless garland of Tapasavi life,
With the message to humanity:
"O my fellow citizens,
In giving, you receive happiness,
In Body and Soul.
You have everything to give.
If you have knowledge, share it.
If you have resources, share them with the needy.
Use your mind and heart,
To remove the pain and the suffering,
And, cheer the sad hearts.
In giving, you receive happiness.
Almighty will bless all your actions.

Creative Leadership

9

Creative Leaders

LEADERS ARE CENTRAL TO ANY major change efforts and we can conclude that transformation equals leadership.

Transformation = Leadership

Without a strong and capable leadership from many people; restructuring, turnarounds and cultural changes either do not happen at all or do not happen effectively. In addition, there is a need to manage the change process in such a way that the operation does not go out of control. A sound managerial support is essential for this. Hence, **highly successful transformation efforts combine good leadership with good management. Such a combination I would call 'creative leadership'.**

CREATIVE LEADERS AT THE TOP OF ENTERPRISES TODAY WILL ENCOURAGE OTHERS TO LEAP INTO THE FUTURE, HELP THEM OVERCOME NATURAL FEARS

AND EXPAND THE LEADERSHIP CAPACITY IN THEIR ORGANISATION. It is a great victory to conquer the peoples' hearts and preserve our democratic traditions.

India has demonstrated its immense capabilities and core-competence to the world with its large talented manpower. It is a nuclear weapon state, self-sufficient in space efforts and defence research, capable of combat technology denial regimes, largest producer of milk, self-sufficient in food, leader in pharmaceuticals, competent in information technology and has large natural resources. What else do we need?

We have such capabilities and strengths in individual domains, but when one looks at India's per capita income we stand at the 105th place in the world.

Why?

What is pulling us down?

What do we need?

We need more and more unique individuals who can be great leaders and managers.

As great leaders and managers will you fill up the vacuum in India and collectively make India reach the highest place?

What should be the purpose of management education?

I think, management education should transform a person into a leader.

Who is a leader?

A leader is the one who thinks what he can GIVE to others instead of expecting what others can do for him.

The second most important thing that a leader needs to have is the ABILITY TO MANAGE AND LEAD THE CHANGE.

What type of change do we mean here?

The entrepreneurs should not be just home grown industrialists but their enterprises should also become leading MNCs.

Leadership with **nobility** and **change management** are the two important elements that the youth need to contribute to the nation.

The nation today, needs a combination of technology and a leadership that uses the technology to bring economic prosperity. The 'developed India', as defined by us, can only be powered by economic strength. The economic strength has to be powered by competitiveness and competitiveness has to be powered by knowledge power. Knowledge power has to be powered by technology and technology has to be powered by innovation and business. Business has to be powered by innovative management and management has to be powered by leadership.

What are the characteristics of leadership? A LEADER NEITHER IS A COMMANDER NOR A SUPER BOSS, BUT HE/SHE IS A VISIONARY, A FACILITATOR OF THE TEAM AND A THINKER. ABOVE ALL, THE NOBILITY OF THE MIND IS THE HALLMARK OF THE LEADER.

- A leader is not a super boss.
- A leader should be ready to give to others rather than expecting others to give him.
- A leader should be equipped to manage change.
- A leader should have nobility of heart.
- A leader should have a vision, capacity to be a facilitator and capability of thinking.

10

Searching the right people and making them grow

Re-entry dynamics!

UNCONNECTED OR IN A CONNECTED way two great scientific minds were responsible for making some unique and beautiful things happen in my life. In 1962, I was working in the Aeronautical Development Establishment (ADE) in the Ministry of Defence as a Senior Scientific Assistant empowered as the leader of the Hovercraft Development Programme. I was responsible for the design, development and also piloting the hovercraft. One day, my director told me that a great scientist was coming to ADE, and that I had to explain to him and give a flight demonstration of the hovercraft. When I met the scientist, I saw in front of me a young bearded, philosopher like personality. He was Prof. M.G.K. Menon, the then Director of Tata Institute of

Fundamental Research. My God, how many questions he asked me in twenty minutes? I took him as a co-passenger in the hovercraft, and gave him a beautiful maneuvered flight on the tarmac.

He loved the flight and congratulated me. I thought that, just like any other VIP visit, this was the end of it. But after a week, I received a telegram (there was no e-mail in those days!) that I must attend an interview for the post of a rocket engineer at the TIFR, Bombay, within a week. My A.D.E. Director helped me to get an airlift one way by taking special permission from the headquarters. I went for that interview. Three people in the interview panel were sitting there, one was Prof. Vikram Sarabhai, I was meeting him for the first time; second was Prof. M.G.K. Menon; and the third was Shri Saraf from the administration. What an interview it was! Prof. Sarabhai asked me questions on what I knew rather than what I didn't know; this was a new way of interviewing. Within an hour, of the interview, I was told that I was selected and my life was steered from Defence to Space Programme.

Another re-entry in my life took place, after the completion of SLV-3 mission. In the year 1981 a lecture series was organized at the Defence Electronics Application Laboratory (DEAL) in Dehradun for presentation of successful technological, scientific programmes of the nation. The first speaker, Dr. Raja Ramanna, the then Scientific Advisor to *Raksha Mantri*, gave a talk on Pokhran nuclear test—technological and management challenges. I was the second speaker and Dr. Raja Ramanna himself presided. The topic I dealt with was the evolution of management system for developing India's first satellite launch vehicle. During the lunch time, Dr. Raja Ramanna asked me to meet him for 10 minutes. I still remember it was 5' O. clock in the evening, on a Sunday in March 1981, the great nuclear scientist Dr. Raja Ramanna told me that he was convinced that I could provide the leadership to the missile programme envisaged by the DRDO. The focal laboratory for the programme was the DRDL. He invited me to become the Director of the DRDL. I was delighted. That was the beginning of the story of my re-entry to defence leading to the evolution of the missile programme. The rest is history. This "great soul" was the Chairman of the Council of IISc and was responsible for guiding the destiny of the Institute for over ten years. ·

Empowering the Young Scientists

I remember an incident with Prof. Vikram Sarabhai during the 1960s. Dr. Sarabhai had nurtured a few scientists and technologists. Let me share with you how he nurtured them. Whenever he came to Trivandrum, I used to discuss with him the proposal for the development of composite products. At that time I was in the initial stages of my career as rocket engineer, with less than two years of experience in ISRO.

Apart from me, there were Dr. S C Gupta, a specialist in guidance and Dr. Amba Rao, a specialist in Aerospace structures. In spite of our being just introduced into the organisation with few years of experience, Dr. Sarabhai noticed our interest in development of certain materials and systems. He funded for the creation of laboratories. He created a fibre composite laboratory based on my proposal, which later became Reinforced Plastic Centre. He created Gyro laboratory centered on the expertise of Dr. Gupta, which later became Guidance Laboratory and Space Structures Laboratory centered around Dr. Amba Rao, which later become advanced dynamics group. These centres became the centres of excellence and incubated many advanced technology missions that fed critical inputs to the space programme.

Once the potential of a young scientist is understood, the heads of the organisation must invest in them boldly irrespective of the position of the scientist and his/her age. If this philosophy is pursued with sincerity the research would flourish and youth would be encouraged to embrace science.

- Leaders with great minds are always looking for the right people to steer a project.
- The right people are self-driven, self-motivated and need no monitoring.
- A high self-concept, his own sense of achievement and grip on the subject makes the selector a positive evaluator, who wants to know what you know and not what you do not know.
- For innovation to flourish, respect the zeal and sincerity irrespective of the age and experience.

Question: What kind of leaders do we need?

Answer: We must generate leaders who say, "What can I do for you"- this is leadership. We need mission-oriented leaders.

11

Development of Creative Leadership

WHAT IS NEEDED TODAY is a combination of TECHNOLOGY, INNOVATION, LEADERSHIP and INSPIRED WORKFORCE for the progress of the nation. Let us analyze the dynamics of good organizations for national development.

- Developed India Can Be Powered Only By Economic Strength.

- The Economic Strength Is Powered By Competitiveness.

- The Competitiveness Is Powered By Knowledge Power.

- The Knowledge Power Is Powered By Technology And Innovation.

- The Technology Is Powered By Resource Investment.

— The Resource Investment Is Powered By Revenue And Return On Investment.

— The Revenue Is Powered By Volume And Repeat Sales Through Customer Loyalty.

— The Customer Loyalty Is Powered By Quality And Value Of Products.

— The Quality And Value Of Products Is Powered By Employee Productivity And Innovation.

— The Employee Productivity Is Powered By Employee Loyalty, Employee Satisfaction And Working Environment.

— The Working Environment Is Powered By Management Leadership.

— The Management Leadership Is Powered By Creative Leadership.

CREATIVE LEADERSHIP IS ONE, WHICH EXERCISES ITS VISION TO CHANGE THE TRADITIONAL ROLE FROM THE COMMANDER TO THAT OF A COACH, FROM THE MANAGER TO MENTOR, FROM DIRECTOR TO DELEGATOR AND FROM THE ONE WHO DEMANDS RESPECT TO THE ONE WHO FACILITATES SELF-RESPECT.

- A true leader does not demand respect but facilitates self-respect of those who work with him.

Question: Sir, you have been closely connected with rocket launching and conquering the sky. What do you think is more meaningful—conquering the sky or conquering the minds?

Answer: It has never been my ambition to conquer the sky or the human mind. My aim has always been to use the strength of each individual human being and their minds for the progress of the nation.

12

Creating Unique Brands

PROMOTING EXCELLENCE IN ORGANIZATIONS which leads to the creation of internationally competitive brand institutions depends on five important components. They are:

1. Design capability,
2. Competitiveness,
3. Organisational transformation,
4. Success/failure management and
5. establishment of Institutional Ethical standards.

Design capability

Technology consists of stages like research and development, technology transfer, technology absorption and production of products or systems with performance, quality and cost effectiveness.

Creation of Internationally Competitive Brands

The indigenous design capability is built through rigorous training in design, development, fabrication and production processes within the country by multiple institutions through appropriate outsourcing and use of available national expertise. It is essential to evolve the value chain in the product life cycle. Wealth generation depends largely on design phase, which contributes about 60 percent of the efforts of development of the product. The quality of the product has to be built-in during the design phase itself. The indigenous design and development capability is the key to acquire a competitive edge. It is very important for the research and development teams, the business community and the industry to recognize the importance of design capability.

The Law of development: Competitiveness

I have been studying the development patterns and the dynamics of connectivity between nations, especially in trade and business. The world has few developed countries and many developing countries. What is the dynamics between them and what connects them? A developed country has to market its products in a competitive way to different countries to maintain its position of a developed country. If a developing country wants to transform into a developed country; they too have to market their products to other countries in a competitive way. Competitiveness has three dimensions:

- Quality of the product
- Cost effectiveness
- On time supply

Product Competitiveness

Indeed, this dynamics of competitiveness in the marketing of products by developing and developed countries is called the law of development.

Organisational transformation

I am sharing with you an experience which has the message on how to transform a 25 year old institution for a new mission.

93

This calls for CHANGING THE OLD ORDER AND SIMULTANEOUSLY EMBEDDING THE NEW MISSION THAT UTILIZES THE TECHNOLOGICAL CORE COMPETENCE OF THE INSTITUTION BY PROVIDING THE RIGHT DIRECTION FOR THE HUMAN POWER. I was the project director of SLV-3 at VSSC, ISRO until 1982. After completing the project, I opted to take up the leadership of Defence Research and Development Laboratory (DRDL) in 1982, for developing the new-generation missile systems. I would like to discuss the birth of a missile programme and the transformation of the laboratory for the new mission. When an institution is nearly 25 years old, as the DRDL was at that time, it has its own ethos and culture and also its pride. The mission of the laboratory was to design, develop and lead missile systems into production. But until 1982, it had not delivered any missile to the armed forces excepting the creation of a technological base, infrastructure and the nurturing of scientific and technical manpower. When I reached the laboratory, one thing was clear to me, the MISSION is the most important component of an institution. All the components of the institution have to be directed to work towards the objective of the laboratory for leading to the development of missiles and production.

Let me summarize the institutional status of the DRDL after two decades from 1982. The DRDL with its partners has now delivered two strategic missile systems for deployment by the Services. These systems are not available for purchase from the international market due to the Missile Technology Control Regime (MTCR) and also due to certain unique performance characteristics needed by our Armed Forces. How was this change brought about?

I ask myself the following questions:

1. Did I bring new leaders from outside the laboratory for the new mission?

   No, not at all.

2. Did I bypass the second line senior scientists and empowered the third line young scientists?

No, never.

3. Was the pride of the laboratory and experienced scientists diminished?

Not, at all.

Yet, how a change was brought about, a change towards a mission oriented organization.

What was the focus?

What was the management style during various phases of the programme?

(i) **Ownership of the programme**

a) During the first year of the programme, the entire scientific community was deployed for making the preliminary design, documents leading to the preparation of the report for the sanctioning of the missile programme by the Government of India and the evolution of a management plan.

b) I remember that about 200 scientists, irrespective of their rank or seniority, worked on this mission without involving any external manpower. When the missile programme was sanctioned at a cost of Rs. 400 crores and a potential to grow to over Rs. 1000 crores, the entire laboratory was proud of this programme and they owned the programme.

c) When the project was sanctioned, the entire laboratory and the external agencies such as 28 work centres and production units participated in the ceremony for the launch of the missile programme presided over by the then Scientific Adviser to the Defence Minister. This one action that the project report was prepared by the laboratory for a great mission of multiple missile development including evolution of production facilities sent a message that the missile programme is a programme of the laboratory and all its work centres. This I consider as the first management step of integrating the minds of workers, staff, scientists and technologists for the ownership of the programme. The message I would like to convey is that always RESPECT THE CORE COMPETENCE OF THE INSTITUTION YOU ARE GOING TO TAKE OVER, VALUE THE PRIDE OF THE PEOPLE AND BUILD ON THEIR STRENGTHS AND CAPABILITIES.

(ii) **Changing the work culture for building indigenous design capability**

Missile Technology Committee for decision making

I started a forum in the laboratory called the Missile Technology Committee (MTC), which met regularly every week on Monday at 14:00 hrs. This MTC was effectively used to elicit different view points on how to cope with the new sanctioned programme of the laboratory, which was bigger than all of us who had assembled there. Two recommendations clearly emerged:

a) The first recommendation was that the DRDL has to become a partner of a number of academic institutions and academicians, who could participate in the design reviews. This led to the establishment of Joint Advanced Technology Programme (JATP) units in Indian Institute of Science, Bangalore and Jadavpur University, Kolkata. This decision resulted in the presence of a number of academic experts in the DRDL campus at all times and as well as the DRDL scientists moving to the academic institutions.

This created a tremendous effect in the minds of the DRDL scientific community that they should acquire knowledge wherever it is available. Thus, for the first time, the DRDL was opened to external knowledge centres which led to the capability enhancement of the laboratory and also building of the confidence among the scientists and technologists, that 'we can do it'. Not only did the laboratory get reinvigorated, the missile programme led to effective management of outsourcing of work to partner laboratories and industries with necessary funding. The DRDL-RCI became a centre of system design, system integration and system management.

b) With the opening of the laboratory to the academic institutions and the partner defence laboratories, the next major decision was to mobilize 300 young scientists from the universities. A special recruitment process was approved for this by the guided missile board, virtually leading to campus recruitment. In six months time all the young scientists were in position in the labs. Once the young scientists came into the scene a new dynamics of enthusiasm and motivation started in the laboratory and multiplied accomplishment of the scientific tasks from the senior scientists.

c) The most important decision taken by the MTC was the establishment of a missile integration centre and test facilities, later called RCI, and the establishment of the missile flight test range. The Guided Missile Board reviewed these requirements and approved them as special programmes with financial empowerment within its own powers. It had never happened in the history of our organization that a large scale technology centre was conceived and established within three years in a green field site through a consultant equipped with high-quality architects and engineers as a turn-key project. Similarly, a new missile flight test range including an island range was established within a record time with the capability of launching multiple missile systems.

The message I would like to convey is that in our country, the Government can empower a programme and enable its completion in record time. It is all about PARTICIPATIVE PROJECT DEFINITION, FULL EMPOWERMENT TO THOSE WHO WILL IMPLEMENT AND OPTIMUM OUTSOURCING TO COMPETENT PARTNERS. This is how, we were able to lead two strategic missiles into production, established two new technological laboratories and a number of production centres in our public sector undertakings and ordnance factories. Also production wings were established in private sector.

(iii) **The Management system for change**

The management system had the following features:

a) The creation of the MTC (Missile Technology Committee) as a technological decision making body.

b) The selection and nomination of five young project directors for the five projects empowered by a management board.

c) Re-organization of the laboratories thrice in ten years: Design phase, Development Phase and Flight trial/ Production phase.

d) The second level senior scientists of the laboratories became technology directors with the accountability to provide all the technological inputs to the projects. These directors became the chairmen of different design review teams.

e) The constitution of a Management Council with all technology directors as members. The project directors were asked to make weekly presentations to the Management

Council, highlighting the progress and problems. The council resolved the inter-project conflicts, provided inter-project priority, suggested resource mobilization strategy and established accountability among all members and the project teams. A healthy working relationship was established among the senior scientists.

f) Constituting a multi-level review system as part of the project and programme management.

The system comprised of:

1. preliminary design review,
2. critical design review,
3. systems review,
4. flight readiness review,
5. post-flight analysis and review and
6. above all a failure review by expert teams.

(iv) **Results of change**

I would like to summarize how we can assess the success of the management system of the missile programme in meeting the objectives set by the government.

a) Capability has been established for the design, development and production of any type of missile without any ambiguity in spite of the MTCR regime.

b) Two strategic missiles went into production and were deployed by the armed forces.

c) Missile development was the territory of one single lab; today there are three labs, 28 partner labs, and two prime production agencies with nearly 20 partner industries.

The successful deployment of the missiles has been possible due to the evolution of design capability, creation of inter-project competitiveness, establishment of a concurrent engineering and production system, creation of multi-tier review mechanism, installation of a robust failure management system, utilization of other institutional capabilities and, above all, an empowered three-tier Guided Missile Management System.

Ethical standards

Organizational ethos comes from traditional leadership. LEADERSHIP COMES FROM THE PROVEN SUCCESSES, FAMILY BACKGROUND, AND ALSO LOVE FOR THE PROGRESS OF THE SOCIETY. The maturity of the quality of leadership is reflected in the transformation from '**you give me**' to '**what I can give you**'. This phenomena is illustrated through an example of my guru Dr. Brahm Prakash. I worked with him during the SLV-3 programme.

When I was the Project Director of the SLV-3 programme, Prof. Brahm Prakash a great scientific leader with nobility, was the Director of Vikram Sarabhai Space Centre(VSSC), which integrated multiple institutions based on the advice of Prof. Kamala Chowdhuri, then a management expert from IIM. Prof Brahm Prakash took hundreds of decisions for the growth of space science and technology.

One great decision I will always cherish. The principle he utilized was: 'once a programme such as SLV-3 is sanctioned the multiple laboratories of Vikram Sarabhai Space Centre and also the multiple centres of ISRO, including the Space Department have to work to realize the stated goals of the programme as a team.' Particularly, during 1973-1980, there was a tremendous financial crunch and competing requirements from many small projects. Prof. Brahm Prakash converged all scientific and technological work to be focused towards SLV-3 and its satellite. Prof. Brahm Prakash is famous for the evolution of management with PURPOSE and NOBILITY, I would like to give a few instances.

He enabled, for the first time, the evolution of a comprehensive management plan for the SLV-3 programme towards the mission of putting the Rohini satellite in orbit. After my task team prepared the SLV-3 management plan, in a period of three months time, he arranged nearly 15 brainstorming meetings of the Space Scientific Committee (SSC). After discussion and approval, this management plan was signed by Prof. Brahm Prakash and became the guiding spirit and working document for the whole organization. This was also the beginning of converting the national vision into mission mode programmes.

During the evolution of the management plan, I could see how multiple views emerged and how, many people being **afraid of losing their individuality due to the main mission, often poured out their anger during the meetings.** I could also see how Prof. Brahm Prakash radiated with a smile in the midst of continuous smoke coming from the cigarettes being lit one after the other. **The anger, fear and prejudice all disappeared in the presence of his nobility of purpose.** Today, the space programme, launch vehicle, spacecraft, scientific experiments and launch missions all are taking place simultaneously in the centres of Indian Space Research Organization(ISRO) in a cohesive and co-operative manner. I remember this great mighty soul who evolved the concept of management with nobility and purpose and created a unique organizational ethos.

He provided the leadership to the 5,000 strong VSSC community with more than 50% of them being scientists at a crucial period after the passing away of Prof Vikram Sarabhai. He led VSSC to success in the mission mode programme with knowledge, technology, and ABOVE ALL WITH HIGH MORAL VALUES.

- Design capability, competitiveness, organisational transformation, success/failure management and establishment of Institutional ethical standards are the cornerstones for creating a brand image.

- Wealth generation depends largely on design phase which contributes about 60% of the efforts of development of the product.

- The quality of the product has to be built in during the design phase itself.

- Competitiveness has three dimensions: quality of the product, cost effectiveness and on time supply.

- It is not changing people but giving them a sense of mission that transforms an institution.

- Always respect the core competence of the institution you are going to take over, value the pride of people and build on their strengths and capability.

- Integrate the minds of workers for owning a programme.

- It is all about participative project definition, full empowerment to those who implement and optimum outsourcing to competent partners.

- We need nobility and purpose to create a unique organizational ethos.

Question: What is the one incident in your past that has left an indelible mark upon you?

Answer: Failure of first SLV launch taught me how to face the failures and how to defeat the problems and succeed. That incident revealed the presence of the leader in the organization.

13

Handling Failure

SUCCESS IS YOURS, FAILURE IS MINE—A real leader's attitude.

I have witnessed several successful flights and a few failures in this range. The first mission was a failure and we recovered fast and we were ready for the second mission. July 18th, 1980 is a memorable day for the entire space community of India. This was the day the space scientists put a 40 kg Rohini satellite in a low earth orbit through SLV–3 (Satellite Launch Vehicle) which took-off at 0805 hrs; within minutes the satellite was in orbit. This was a great accomplishment for our scientists, especially after the unsuccessful earlier mission on August 10th, 1979.

There was jubilation all around. People were thrilled. They were shouting, hugging and lifting each other and were emotionally charged. This was the time Prof. Dhawan took me aside and said that we should go to a silent place. Both of us went to the launch pad and sat on the launcher. We watched the waves of the Bay of Bengal in silence. After a few minutes, Prof. Dhawan said to me: "Kalam, you know you have been working hard for the last eight years. You encountered a number of problems and failures. You faced them all with utmost courage, patience and perseverance. For all the efforts that you put in, today we have got the results. I want to thank you for your excellent work. I will remember and cherish it." I had never come across such a beautiful day till then. In the din of loud external jubilation of the entire space community, Prof. Dhawan and I were enjoying the intrinsic beauty of the mega event.

Failure Management

Two decades ago, while I was working at ISRO, I had the best of education, which could not have been received from any university.

I will narrate that incident. I was given a task by Prof. Satish Dhawan, the then Chairman, ISRO, to develop the first satellite launch vehicle SLV-3 to put Rohini satellite in orbit. This was one of the largest high-technology space programmes undertaken in1973. The whole space technology community, both men and women, were geared up for this task. Thousands of scientists, engineers and technicians worked for the realization of the first SLV-3 launch. The first SLV-3 experimental launch was planned to take-off at 1500 hrs. on August10th, 1979. I as the Mission Director, was in the SHAR Control Centre along with a 50 member strong team with six specialists to assist me in critical decision-making before the take-off.

The automated computer count stopped indicating a possible anomaly in the propulsion system. My specialist team saw on the display that in the second stage of flight, the pressure dropped in the reaction control system oxidiser tank that provides the three axis altitude control after the first-stage rocket is separated. The specialist team advised me to go ahead with the countdown ignoring the pressure drop as they felt that the propellant stored was sufficient enough to last for twice the flight duration. I was advised to go ahead with the launch. I concurred and pushed the computer button to the launch sequence.

At T-0 the SLV-3 took off beautifully. The first stage had given predicted thrust and altitude and velocity needed at given altitude.

The second stage initiated as per the tele-data, but within a few seconds, we witnessed the second stage and third stage, and the satellite got caught into a tumbling motion, and we lost the flight to the Bay of Bengal. It was 7 am in the morning. The whole team, in spite of all its day-and-night hard work prior to the launch, were busy in collecting the data and was trying to establish the reason for the flight failure.

Meanwhile, I was called by Prof Satish Dhawan to attend a press conference. Before the press conference, Prof. Satish Dhawan told me he was going to handle the situation and I should be present with many of the senior scientists and technologists. And there he announced that he took the responsibility for not achieving the mission, even though I was the project director and the mission director. The press conference room was full with media. There was gloom, many questions were posed, some very powerful, thoughtful also criticisms. Prof. Satish Dhawan announced: "Friends, today we had our first satellite launch vehicle to put satellite in the orbit, we could not succeed. It was our first mission of proving multiple technologies in satellite launch vehicles. In many technologies we have succeeded and in a few more we have to succeed. Above all I realize my team members will have to be given all the technological support. I am going to do that and in the next mission we will succeed." Subsequently, a failure analysis board was formed to establish the cause.

When we launched SLV-3 on July 18th, 1980, successfully injecting Rohini satellite into the orbit, again there was a press conference and

Prof. Dhawan put me in the front to share the success story with the press. What we learn from this event is that a leader takes the responsibility of failure but gives the credit of the success to the team members

This is the leadership. The scientific community in India has had the fortune to work with such leaders because of whom so many accomplishments have been possible.

- A Leader takes the responsibility of failure but gives the credit of success to the team members.

106

14

Defeat the Problems and Succeed

I WANT TO SHARE WHAT I FELT after the Columbia's tragedy. Human flight is nothing but the creativity of human mind and it undergoes several struggles to achieve excellence by exploring the space.

In 1890, a well-known scientist Lord Kelvin, who was the President of Royal Society of London said, "Any thing heavier than air cannot fly, and cannot be flown." With in two decades Wright Brothers proved that man can fly, of course, at a heavy risk and cost.

On the successful completion of Moon Mission in 1961, Farnbraun, a very famous rocket designer, who built Saturn-V, to launch the capsule with astronauts and made the moon walk a reality said, "If I am authorized, I will remove the word impossible from the dictionary." Now let us take the story of the planet earth. During the recent Columbia's space mission, on January 29, 2002 at 3.39 PM, the astronauts M.C Cool & Ramon said to the ground station, "We are in a vantage point in space, the world looks marvelous from up here, so peaceful, so wonderful and so fragile... ." Those seven astronauts are no more with us. They have given so much of scientific inputs to the humanity. In addition, they have given a very important message that the earth is fragile.

In ancient days, Ptolemaic astronomy was a widely used system for calculating the dynamics of various stars and planets.

The assumption then was that the earth is flat. What a scientific struggle had to take place to prove that the earth is spherical in shape orbiting around the sun. The two great astronomers, Copernicus and Galileo had to give a new dimension to the world of astronomy. Galileo was jailed for his discovery.

Today, we take it for granted that earth is a globe orbiting around the sun and the sun orbits in the Milky Way. All the technological advancements we have today are the outcome of scientific explorations of scientists of past few centuries. At no time, was man beaten by problems. He strives continuously to subjugate failures. Our tributes to those seven astronauts who lost their lives in Columbia. Such thoughts are meant to tell us that failures should not deter our steps towards progress.

- Failures should not deter our steps towards progress.

Question: Who guides you in your stressful moments?

Answer: I remember my Gurus such as Satish Dhawan, who always said when you do work there will always be problems, what is important is that you must defeat the problems and overcome them.

15

Don't fear failure
Don't fear crisis

A Personal crisis may change history

My Search For Bringing together Peace and prosperity

SOMETIMES I INTENTLY THINK, what can bring peace and prosperity together. I have visited all parts of our country and talked to the children, the youth and the experienced. I have also visited several countries in three continents. When I addressed the Pan-African Parliament represented by 53 African countries, I happened to meet the heads of state of these countries and their citizens. These meetings triggered many random thoughts in me. I would like to share

with you how the Father of our Nation, Mahatma Gandhi, working at Durban in South Africa, experienced the insult and humiliation under the apartheid regime and fought back during the period 1893-1914. This later on led to the birth of non-cooperation movement through non-violence. During my visit to South Africa in 2004, I boarded a train at Penrich railway station near Durban for a journey to Pietermaritzburg, just tracing the footsteps of Mahatma Gandhi.

It was from Durban station that Mahatma had embarked on the fateful journey that in later years is regarded as having changed the course of his life. He boarded the train on June 7, 1893 in order to travel to Pretoria, where he was due to meet legal clients. A first-class seat was booked for him. The train reached Pietermaritzburg station at about 9.00 p.m. A White passenger entering the compartment could not stomach coloured person travelling with him. So he went out and returned with two officials who ordered Gandhiji to move to the van compartment. When Gandhiji resisted as he had the valid

110

ticket to travel in that compartment, a white constable was called who took Gandhiji by hand and pushed him out of the train. His luggage was also thrown out, and the train continued its journey without him. Gandhiji spent the night in the waiting room. It was winter, and the weather was bitterly cold. Although his overcoat was in the luggage, Gandhiji did not ask for it fearing further insults. Gandhiji contemplated returning to India but decided that such a course would be cowardice. He vowed to stay and fight the disease of racial prejudice. This changed the course of his life. Gandhiji even said, "... my active non-violence began from that date."

The train and the compartments in which we travelled were exactly same compartments in which the Mahatma had travelled. When I got down at the Pietermaritzburg station, I saw the plaque in whose vicinity the Mahatma was thrown out. I also went to the waiting- room where Mahatma had spent the cold wintry night. The action of Mahatma Gandhi his courage when he was insulted by the White constable later led to the birth of *Ahimsa Dharma*. This was the first movement in South Africa against racial discrimination. The people of South Africa remember the courageous action of Mahatma Gandhi, and as a nation, they are grateful to him. The fight against apartheid in South Africa at that time was indeed an experience for Mahatma Gandhi. It became a precursor to India's freedom movement.

I also recall, the connectivity with the Kalinga war scene, about 2300 years back, where Emperor Ashoka's mind transformed, while celebrating the victory in the Kalinga war, at the cost of the death of more than one hundred thousand people and an equal number injured. In his victory, the emperor saw the bloodbath in the moonlit night. Here, we see the birth of *Ahimsa Dharma*, out of this tragic scene created by the Emperor himself grow into a laudable philosophy that spread across the world.

A long walk to Freedom

I would also like to share with you the scene in the Robben Island of Atlantic Ocean. In this scene, I see an indomitable spirit of Dr. Nelson Mandela, who was jailed for 26 years in a single prison cell. When he was freed, he gave two great gifts to his nation. One was the magnanimity in victory by providing equal constitutional rights to the 10% of the White population, who were the main propagators of apartheid. The second was his book entitled—*A long walk to freedom,* the famous work which he wrote stealthily in the prison. With all my experience in India and abroad, one thing is very clear, that in

this planet of 6 billion people, what is needed is the **fight against injustice**. Mahatma Gandhi in Africa fought against apartheid, Dr. Nelson Mandela gave the final leadership to remove the apartheid regime from South Africa. In India, Gandhiji with his experience in fighting against injustice in South Africa, fought against the British for India's freedom. FROM THESE EXPERIENCES, WHAT WE LEARN HISTORICALLY IS THAT WE HAVE TO HAVE A MAJOR MISSION AGAINST INJUSTICE AND WE HAVE TO FIGHT TILL INJUSTICE IS COMPLETELY REMOVED.

Shape of Injustice

What is that injustice? The injustice that we have to fight today is the societal and economic impoverishment and inequality in various aspects of life for a large number of people. India's movement in removing this impoverished state will become a trendsetter for the whole planet. When India got its freedom in 1947, many nations in Asia and Africa were inspired to fight for freedom and were able to achieve freedom for their nations. Thus as in the past, now again India will be able to lead in releasing the people all over the world from the shackles of injustice. When would India become a developed nation, and show the way to the other developing nations? Will history repeat itself?

Yes, it will be possible by the youth power—half the population of India.

- Don't fear failure—a personal crisis may bring a turning point in life which may change the course of life for the better—or may even change history.
- Have a major mission against injustice — the injustice of social and economic impoverishment.

113

16

Courage, Commitment and Endurance

AS A LEADER WE NEED TO passionately own our mission. This brings the courage for making any sacrifice for it. We also need presence of mind and strong nerves. Here are two examples.

At every stage of its development, the SLV–3 team was blessed with some extraordinarily courageous people. Shri Sivakaminathan was bringing the C-band transponder[1] from Trivandrum to SHAR for integration with SLV–3. The SLV–3 launch schedule was dependent on the arrival and integration of this equipment. On landing at the Madras(Chennai) airport, the aircraft in which Sivakami was travelling skidded and overshot the runway. Dense smoke engulfed the aircraft. Everyone jumped out of the aircraft through the emergency exit and

---

1. Transponder is an airborne instrument that helps the radar to track the missile thousands of kilometers.

desperately fought to save him/herself—all except Sivakami who stayed in the aircraft till he removed the transponder from his baggage. He was among the last few persons to emerge from the smoke, holding the transponder close to his chest. This is the level of dedication and the attachment to the project, which gives courage to make any sacrifice.

Another incident happened during the third launch of SLV-3. The count down sequence was proceeding smoothly. There were two operations to be carried out on the launcher—one for the release of the spacecraft umbilical and the other for the release of the arms holding the vehicle. Both these were pneumatically operated systems remotely controlled from Block House. The arms got released as expected. However, the spacecraft umbilical release system failed to respond to the command. This put on hold the countdown automatically. There was a suspense on how to go about, and the launch managers huddled together to find a solution. Shri M.R. Kurup and I volunteered to reach the umbilical system through a ladder to manually release it. Seeing the situation, one young tradesman of SHAR, Shri Pappaiah, volunteered to climb on to the launcher and release the mechanism manually. After clearance by the concerned, he accomplished this marvelous feat, and the vehicle was launched that day. I can never forget such committed individuals who have been the backbone of ISRO.

Experience in a full moon night

I would like to tell another small and funny incident which I experienced when I was working with DRDO (1999). It was a full moon night on the Wheeler Island. We launched the operationalized version of Agni.

The launch was a textbook launch and the mission requirements were fully met, and the re-entry vehicle went exactly to the target. It was a day of great joy. After the first phase of the post-flight analysis,

I had to rush to Dhamra, then to Chandipur and next-day morning to Calcutta(Kolkata) so that I could reach for the LCA review at Bangalore. I was going in a powered boat from the Wheeler shore to the Dhamra shore, a ride which normally takes 40 minutes. Dr. S.K. Salwan, Shri S.C. Narang and I were enjoying the ride on a full moon night. The sea was very rough. The waves were rocky, and cold and salty water was being sprayed on us. To our great surprise, midway from Wheeler Island to Dhamra, the engine of our boat stopped functioning. Imagine an engineless boat with no sails, on a full moon night, and when even the sea is very rough. The rocky waves were showing their strength by hitting on our boat. Except the boatmen and me none of the others could swim. Everybody was frightened. When people were afraid and jittery about what is going to happen, I had to keep their minds busy and free from fear. So, I started telling them my experiences with the sailboat that my father had built for ferrying the pilgrims from Rameshwaram to Dhanushkodi. As a small boy, I was given the job of continuously emptying the water from the boat, which used to come inside due to the leakage from wooden hull. For emptying the water during to and from journey, I used to get a bonus of one *anna*. This experience gave a sense of happiness to my colleagues. Meanwhile, using the boat's communication, we could contact the other boat, which reached us after a short while. All of us got ourselves transferred to the new boat and reached Dhamra. This was a good test of endurance.

- Commitment to the mission gives courage to recover it even at the peril of one's life.

116

Question: How did you feel when you were declared as President-designate?

Answer: I thought about my parents and my teachers who inspired me to work and make contribution to the society. Above all a feeling in me echoed, "What can I give to the people of my nation."

17

Passion, Creativity and Innovation

The strength of an enterprise

WHAT IS NEEDED IN ACHIEVING GREATNESS for an institution is not only knowledge, but also people with passion. **This passion should not be limited to the technical aspects but should also aim towards creating a concern for the society with a view to finding positive solutions to the problems faced by the people.** We need leaders who can create such passion among our youth and channel their vibrant energy to make the nation competitive. What are the methods of achieving this?

Thrust for indigenous technology

Technology is a non–linear tool that can effect the most fundamental change in the ground rules of economic competitiveness. Technology consists of stages like research and development, technology transfer, technology absorption, and production of products or systems with the desired performance, quality and cost-effectiveness. Technology development can be achieved through two routes—Route A and Route B. Route A *(know-how)* involves obtaining licensed technology or techniques, including manufacturing, design drawings, and production processes from an established manufacturer from abroad. Route B *(know-why)* begins with designing and developing indigenous technology. In the case of India, progress in technology, particularly indigenous design, is the thrust area to enable India to become competitive with other countries.

Creativity—Mining the minds

Since our population is of a billion people in India, the society in its own way has to innovate continuously, not only in urban but also in rural areas. For example, the honeybee network movement is indeed an excellent attempt. Creativity comes from beautiful minds. It can be anywhere and in any part of the country. It may start from a fisherman's hamlet or a farmer's household or a dairy farm or cattle breeding centre, or it may emanate from classrooms, laboratories, industries or R & D centres. Creativity has got multiple dimensions like inventions, discoveries and innovations. It can imagine or invent something new by combining, changing or reapplying existing ideas. Creativity has an attitude to accept change and newness, a willingness to play with ideas and possibilities, a flexibility of outlook, the habit of enjoying the good, while looking for ways to improve it. Creativity has a process to work hard and to improve ideas and solutions continuously by making gradual alterations and refinements to their works.

The important aspect of creativity is—seeing the same thing as everybody else, but thinking of something different. Imagination generates creativity, creativity leads to thinking.

Innovation

There is a need to nurture innovation at our workplaces. Innovation is market driven. Innovation can also be in the form of improving performance of the product/system technique by adopting a change using alternative technologies. Science is linked to technology through applications. Technology is linked to economy and environment through manufacturing. Economy and environment link technology to society. So, there is an integrated relationship between science, technology, environment, manufacturing and society.

Building innovation systems

It is through the process of innovation that knowledge is converted into wealth and social good. Further, innovation is an important factor for the competitiveness of both service and manufacturing sectors. Innovation tends to emanate less from R & D and more from other sources, including organizational change. Hence, there is an urgent need to establish an efficient innovation system in the country. Such a system would involve the creation of clusters, which are networks of inter-dependent firms, knowledge producing institutions (universities, colleges/institutes, research institutes, technology providing firms), and bridging institutions (e.g. think-tanks, providers of technical or consultancy services) and customers linked in a value-addition creating a production chain.

The concept of clusters goes beyond that of a firm network, as it captures all forms of knowledge sharing and exchange. Thus an innovation system with its clusters would tap into the growing stock of global knowledge, assimilate and adapt it to local needs and finally create new knowledge and technology. For such an innovation system to succeed, the following points are necessary: (a) improve inter-ministerial coordination and ensure consistency and credibility in policy formulation; and (b) introducing new mechanisms to support innovation and technology diffusion, including greater use of public/private partnership.

Innovation is the capital

The Global Competitiveness Report for the year 2003-04 shows that in terms of Growth Competitive Index ranking US is ranked 2nd, Singapore 6th, South Africa 42nd, China 44th, and India 56th. In the same report, I noticed that in the proportion of Scientists and Engineers Index US ranked 4th, Singapore 6th, South Africa 38th, China 43rd and India 60th. Thus, we can see that there is a close correlation between the growth competitive index and the scientists and engineers index who are the innovators for the organization.

This innovation arises from the institutional initiative and the R & D productivity of the firm, shaped by policies and nature of local institutions. THE NATIONAL INNOVATIVE CAPACITY HAS TO BE THE COUNTRY'S IMPORTANT POTENTIAL TO REINFORCE BOTH POLITICAL AND ECONOMIC ENTITY WITH COMMERCIALLY RELEVANT COMPETITIVE PRODUCTS. This capacity is distinct from purely scientific or technical achievements and focuses on the economic application of new technology.

Kancheepuram Story

The silk industry in Kancheepuram is one of the fastest-growing industries in India. The industry currently employs more than 30,000 weavers in the art of *saree* making. The industry had to compete with the synthetic fiber industry in many aspects, and it was on the brink of extinction due to the obsolescence of the designs and design making procedures. Because, design adds splendour to a *saree* and forms an integral part of its exquisiteness. This may also be true for many handloom *saree* producers in different parts of the country.

The introduction of computerized Jacquard border design in Kancheepuram silk *saree* has helped in the revival of the industry. The use of computer-aided design has not only helped in creating new and complex designs but has also reduced the time involved in producing the design. There has been an increase in the exports.

The acceptance of these silk *sarees* by the consumers has also increased with the automation of designing process. The Visualization of *saree* design ahead of its production and the ability to create new colour combinations at the click of a mouse has increased the flexibility and reduced the time for realizing new designs. Though the materials and the techniques are changing with the market demand, the motifs are still conventional to maintain the custom and tradition of the Kancheepuram *saree*. The silk industry in Kancheepuram has transformed into a high-growth industry by opening up new avenues for the traditional weavers. The example illustrates that computer-aided design can help the renewal of a traditional industry provided the new technology is simple to use, and the users are trained compatible with the traditional manufacturing process properly.

- The national innovative capacity is a country's important potential.
- It focuses on the economic application of new techonology.
- Creative utilisation of new technology can help the renewal of traditional industry.

Question: Your Excellency, which was the proudest moment of your life?

Answer: The proudest moment in my life was when a polio affected child who was walking with great difficulty using a four Kg Floor Reaction Orthosis (callipers for polio affected children), was provided with a light-weight FRO weighing 400 grams using carbon fibre used in defence equipment. The child started jumping, running and riding a bicycle. Her parents shed tears of joy. I was in real bliss.

18

Developing Special Leadership Styles

IN THE PRESENT ENVIRONMENT, we require new leadership styles; namely, politics for development, administration for economic growth, banking for entrepreneur creation and Indian business for global market share.

Politics for development will require a leadership style which will stimulate and enable the reaching of prosperity to people. There should be competition to bring connectivity to rural areas, to bring new investment and to bring new knowledge and skills to the people. It will be the leadership which will explain the new opportunities to people at large and make them work in the right direction.

When I was reading the speeches of the first President of the country Dr. Rajendra Prasad, in the Rashtrapati Bhavan Library, I was inspired and got the message for all of us in our country—various constitutional functionaries, including the judiciary. Dr. Rajendra Prasad, as chairman of Constituent Assembly on 26th November 1949, when it met to approve the draft constitution prepared by Dr. Ambedkar, in his concluding speech observed that, on the whole they had been able, to draft a good constitution which he trusted would serve the country well. He added:

"If the people who are elected are capable and men of character and integrity, they would be able to make the best even of a defective constitution. If they are lacking in these, the constitution cannot help the country. After all, a constitution like a machine is a lifeless thing. It acquires life because of men who control it and operate it, and India needs today nothing more than a set of honest men who will have the interest of the country before them." The administrative leaders for development will support the political development leaders and remove the impediments coming in the way of economic and social growth. Their job should be to remove hurdles and hassles for citizens and investors.

Financial service leadership is required for an all-round economic growth. It has to cater to the needs of the big businesses. In India to achieve multinational leadership, it should provide quick and efficient service for mega projects, which should also be innovative to support aspiring young boys and girls possessing knowledge and skills to start new, risky enterprises with great potential. Financial service leaders in the new era should develop new skills, which will enable even a poor farmer to acquire new skills and to invest in new methods of work in agriculture and agro-processing, including IT services. The business leaders for developed India have to discard the old mind-set, think big on the global scale, look for an order of magnitude, higher global market share and aim to enhance the Indian GDP to double digits. They should also create world-class ancillaries around them, transforming our small and medium enterprises into global leaders. In essence, the business leaders of developed India should aim at making the country a global granary of high-value food and agriculture products, the world's manufacturing base and a multi-continent service leader.

Creative Leadership

What I learnt from Prof. Satish Dhawan, a former Chairman of ISRO is a great message for the young and aspiring students. I worked with Prof Satish Dhawan for a decade, particularly in the development of the first satellite launch vehicle programme for which I was fortunate to have been chosen as the Project Director. Prof. Satish Dhawan, gave the country, great leadership values which we may not find in any management book. He taught me a lot through his personal example. When a mission is progressing, there will always be some problems or failures, but the failures should not become the master of the programme. The leader has to subjugate the problem, defeat the problem and has to lead the team to success. This knowledge became embedded in me right from those days and has stood by me throughout my life.

Leaders for knowledge society

I consider, until the year 2020, a period of technological transformation of India. I anticipate new emerging economic and technical situations where many new technologies will emerge to help country's development. India is now standing at the gate of the knowledge society and with our skill development in the field of information technology. What we need is a little of an entrepreneurial push and an increase in our competitiveness. With these tools, we will be prepared to take on the new trends, with minimal government interference and support, and we would be able to hold our head high and stand among the internationally developed countries of the world. My experience of working has shown that we need role models who will ignite the minds of the young people. I appeal to all the business and political leaders to play a key role in developing the minds and vision of youth of today. They look up to the leaders as role models for their future and if we are successful in igniting their minds, we would have done a great service for the state as well as for the nation.

Spiritual Leadership to Clean the environment

The status of environmental cleanliness is one of the indicators of the development of a nation. As a nation, we have to keep our environment clean, including all our rivers and places of worship. Cleaning of Kali Bein, in Panjab, is an example of preservation of environment through spiritual leadership. I am delighted to learn that the Kali Bein rivulet, the place where Sri Gurunanak Dev is said to have received enlightenment, and which had over the centuries turned literally into a sewage-ridden, weed-choked drain, is today flowing clean and proud due, mainly to the efforts of Baba Balbir Singh Seechewal in partnership with the Panjab State Government. I understand that he organized people's participation in stopping the massive flow of sewage into the Bein and cleaned the 160 km long polluted and choked rivulet within the last three and a half years by deploying, on an average, 3000 devotees per day of the Gurudwara, who have become volunteer workers for the mission. Today, one can feel the flow of fresh water in this rivulet released from the Tarkina Barrage. The revival of the rivulet has recharged the water table as the hand-pumps that had become dry for the past four decades are now pumping out water. Baba, with the volunteers, not only did the cleaning up operation by clearing Bein from the weeds and hyacinth, but also built bathing ghats at five places and built more than 100 km long kutcha road on the bank of the rivulet.

Leaders for Education—minimizing school dropout

Prof. M.R. Raju lives in his native village Peddamiram, close to Bheemavaram, Andhra Pradesh. The life of Prof. Raju is indeed exemplary. A famous nuclear scientist working in Los Alamos Laboratory, USA, Prof. Raju, left his job and returned to his village.

He decided to transform Peddamiram and its surroundings with the support of his family members. With his assets, he started the Mahatma Gandhi Memorial Medical Trust in that village. In a decade, he and his team, supported by volunteers from various institutions from India and abroad, have brought a great change to the people in his village.

He particularly targeted character building and uplifting of the children in the age group of three to five years. The village has 100 children in this age group, out of which 50 belong to the high-income group and study in private schools. The 30 children who are very poor, they study in the Balawadi School run by the State Government. The other 20 have joined the school being run by Prof. Raju. In this school, the parents have to pay a fee of half a day's wages per child per month. For girl students, they have to pay Rupees 10 per month. The emphasis in this school is on playful environment, nutritional support and caring love. This experiment is being repeated in many other schools. The parents are periodically invited to the school and given training on the need for providing nutrition to the children through proteins, leafy vegetables and eggs. The children are given training on cleanliness and hygiene. With this training, they become teachers at home for hygienic practice and do not allow unhygienic practices by any of their members. When the teachers interact with the children, they always talk to them to develop the scientific attitude. This technique is promoting creativity among the children. The children are encouraged to give their own answers as they feel rather than giving stereotyped premeditated answers. For example, when a child is shown the letter 'B' and asked what he understands by this letter, the child may say it looks like a spectacle instead of the usual answer 'B'. Similarly, when a sketch is started with some features such as eyes or lips, the children are able to draw a full picture.

This shows the creative ability of the students. These students once trained in Prof Raju's school for three years learn to enjoy studies and do not become dropouts later. This has totally transformed the village atmosphere and the dropout rate of the children in schools has come down substantially. A confident young population is emerging in the village and its surroundings. This method of training,which is being practiced by Prof Raju and his team for the last 10 years, has been researched by child psychologists and educational theorists. This approach makes the child a willing learner before entering the school and makes him to participate in the school learning process when he/she joins the regular school.

- Political leadership style should aim at making prosperity reach the poorest sectors of society.
- Business leaders should aim at creating global leadership in their field.
- Spiritual leaders can help in social and environmental causes.
- Leaders for a knowledge society should encourage quality and competitiveness.

19

Team building

MOST OF THE DISCOVERIES AND INNOVATIONS are team efforts. Education system should work towards team building among the students. Every student must have an opportunity to play the role of a team member and a team leader so that he can see both sides of the fence. The amount of information that we have around us is overwhelming. The management of knowledge, therefore, must move out of the realm of the individual and shift into the realm of the networked groups. The students must learn how to manage knowledge collectively. When the information is networked, the power and utility of the information grows as squared, as predicted by Metcalfe's law. Information that is static does not grow. In the new digital economy, information that is circulated creates innovation and contributes to national wealth. The importance of team building increases in this context.

First lessons in team building

How did I get my first lessons in team building? During the final year of aeronautical engineering course, I was given a six-month project for developing a low-level attack aircraft along with six of my class mates. We divided the work in our team. One person studied propulsion and engine selection, the second studied the aircraft structures and materials, the third looked at the control system, fourth studied the aerodynamic design and two of us were responsible for the integration of multiple systems, culminating in an integrated aircraft to meet the performance requirements. This task became for me the foundation for learning to work with a team in an integrated way and to evolve system engineering and system management concepts. Prof. Wrepenthin, was responsible for designing such a project for the students.

Creative Use of Materials and team effort

FRO, Floor Reaction Orthosis is a walking aid for the polio-affected children. In 1983, its conventional version was introduced in India by Prof. P K Sethi of Jaipur and Prof S C Lakkad of IIT, Bombay. In the early 1990s, the doctors from Nizam's Institute of Medical Sciences, (NIMS), Hyderabad, contacted me and asked if the high technologies of defence could be used for medical science. They brought to the fore the specific problem of polio appliances, which are required in great numbers but the conventional method of their fabrication could not produce enough to match the requirement in the country. Moreover, they felt that there was a need to improve upon the materials and quality of the appliances. Immediately, the advanced composite materials, used in the fabrication of missile airframes, which are quite light weight and very strong came to my mind. I thought if they could be used for the fabrication of light-weight, ultra-strong and durable standardized walking aids. The standardization was the only way to mass produce these walking aids in order to meet the demand.

Then, a team consisting of scientists from the DRDO and doctors from NIMS was asked to make the detailed study of the problem and, later, a project was sanctioned jointly by Department of Science and Technology and the Ministry of Social Justice and Empowerment.

Standardisation

The project team consisted of doctors, orthotists, plastic engineers, mechanical engineers and software engineers. An equipment, namely Anthropometric Measuring Device for generating data on polio affected lower limbs, was invented and data on more than 1000 polio-affected limbs was generated through various polio camps all over the country. This data was analyzed by specially developed software programme, namely FROSTAN.

After the analysis, a modular concept with standard sizes was evolved leading to three modules namely foot piece, knee piece and a pair of lateral uprights. The materials chosen for the fabrication for these modules were E-glass reinforced polypropylene composites and these modules were produced through injection moulding and compression moulding technologies. The local industries at Hyderabad participated in the initial phase of the production and trials. The trial fitment was carried out on over 500 polio-affected children in various parts of India. The response of these children was overwhelming and the feedback obtained was heartening. The doctors and orthotists were delighted to have a polio appliance which met all their expectations in terms of quality, affordability, light weight and durability.

The standardization of sizes and use of the sate-of-the-art materials and technologies made FRO a high quality and cost-effective walking aid, which met the expectations of the needy children, doctors and orthotists. The complete technology was transferred to M/s. ALIMCO, Kanpur for mass production. Presently, ALIMCO is mass producing it and this appliance has been taken abroad too, by ALIMCO. Floor

Reaction Orthosis is available for Rupees 300 and weighs as less as 300 gm. It can be fitted onto a needy child in less than an hour.

Kalam-Raju stent

I was traveling in a non-stop train from Delhi to Dehradun, absorbed in a book "Man, the Unknown" written by Dr. Alexis Carell. There was a vacant seat next to me. Suddenly one passenger greeted me. He wanted to convey something to me. I asked him to sit by my side. He introduced himself and said he is working in a government office. His name was Jitesh. Mr Jitesh said, "Mr. Kalam, I want to thank you for giving to people like me Raju-Kalam stents which are fitted in two of my arteries. I was fitted with these stents in Hyderabad Hospital almost at no cost, since at that time, I could not afford a high cost imported stent." Raju-Kalam stent emanated through the working of missile lab and medical institution on a mission mode. It was a successful mission of medical and engineering teams. I thought of sharing this incident with you to stress the importance of medical and engineering teams to work together for developing medical systems, devices and equipments at an affordable cost as a societal mission.

Dr. Soma Raju is one of the founding members of society for biomedical technology (SBMT), an inter-ministerial initiative of the Government of India to develop affordable medical devices and technology. We made a coronary stent together. The KR stent, as it was called, resulted in the availability of all international brands of coronary stents in India at the most nominal prices.

The Amul Cooperative model

The cooperative model of Amul is one of the leading examples of the successful cooperative model in 20th century in the country. The effort of Dr. V. Kurien, the pioneer of this movement, has made India a leading producer of milk and milk products.

A white revolution was introduced in the country through the comprehensive dairy development project undertaken with an outlay of over Rupees 1700 crores in three phases. This project was financed through the community aid programme and loans from World Bank and was implemented during the period 1970-1996. This programme has enriched over eleven million farmer members. It has covered over one lac village cooperative societies set up under the umbrella of 170 district cooperative milk unions, resulting in the production of over 110 lac kg of milk per day. This has resulted in self-sufficiency of milk and milk products in the country, enriching the farmers and giving a new dimension to this sector.

The project is growing continuously. One important feature of the project is that the increase in productivity of milk has not resulted in the reduction in the per litre price of milk. This is because of the milk being converted into innovative dairy products needed to meet the growing demand of the nation. For the success of the projects we need to ensure that these programmes are speedily implemented so that their benefits can reach all the members of the rural community within a definite time frame of ten years. With our experience in the cooperative sector, this should be possible.

A Great mind and a great heart go together

Nobel Laureate Prof. Norman E. Borlaug, a well known agricultural scientist and a partner in India's first Green revolution, was being conferred Dr. M S Swaminathan Award, at Vigyan Bhavan, New Delhi on the 15th of March 2005. Prof. Borlaug, who was 91 years old, was showered praise on him from everybody gathered there. When Prof. Borlaug's turn to address the gathering came, he highlighted India's advancement in agricultural science and production and said that the political visionary Shri C. Subramaniam and Dr. M S Swaminathan were the prime architects of the first Green

Revolution in India. He also recalled with pride Dr. Verghese Kurien who ushered White Revolution in India. Then the surprise came. He turned to the scientists sitting in the third row, fifth row and eighth row of the audience. He identified Dr. Raja Ram, a wheat specialist, Dr. S K Vasal, a maize specialist, Dr. B. R. Barwale, a seed specialist and said, all these scientists had contributed to India's and Asia's agricultural science. Dr. Borlaug introduced them to the audience by asking them to stand and ensured that the audience cheered and greeted the scientists with great enthusiasm. Such a scene I had not witnessed in our country before. I call this action of Dr. Norman Borlaug, as Scientific Magnanimity. IF WE ASPIRE GREATNESS, WE NEED MAGNANIMITY. IT IS MY EXPERIENCE THAT A GREAT MIND AND A GREAT HEART GO TOGETHER.

This Scientific Magnanimity motivates the scientific community and nurtures the team spirit. I am reminded of Thiruvalluvar's famous Thirukkural; which implies that right thoughts become seeds for great achievements.

Leaders are the creators of new organizations of excellence. Quality leaders are like magnets that attract the best people to build the team for the organization and provide inspiring leadership even during failures of individuals or organizations as they are not afraid of risks.

- We should learn to work in a team, both as a leader and as a member of the team.
- A great mind and a great heart go together.
- Most of the successful projects are possible only with a team effort.
- We should have magnanimity to accept and appreciate the efforts and achievements of others.

20

Self-reliance

THE COUNTRY NEEDS A CHANGE IN the mindset of the people. Certain people have a mentality that only a system or product from cosmetics to cars, electronic items to defence equipment, if of foreign origin will be better and so is preferable. I can understand the import of these items if India does not want to make or does not have the capability to produce them. We should also export what we make in large quantities or what we make out of our core competence. If India has to achieve technological strength, self-reliance in Indian products and Indian systems has to grow in the minds of the people. This change of mind is indeed revolutionary. Women, the world over, have been known as excellent and efficient change agents. I would request particularly women scientists to propagate this revolutionary thought in self-reliance in the homes, laboratories, industrial establishments or wherever they work. A self-reliant nation should indeed be a mission for all of us.

Knowledge in network society

A knowledge society can be one of the foundations for the vision of a Developed and self-reliant India. Knowledge has many forms and is available at many places. Knowledge has always been the prime mover of prosperity and power. The acquisition of knowledge has therefore been the thrust area throughout the world and sharing the experience of knowledge is a unique feature of the culture of our country. India is a nation endowed with natural and competitive advantages as also certain distinctive competencies. But these are scattered in isolated pockets and the awareness on these is inadequate. During the last century, the world has changed from being an agricultural society, where manual labour was the critical factor, to an industrial society where the management of technology, capital and labour provided the competitive advantage. Then the information era was born, in the last decade, connectivity and software products are driving the economy of a few nations. In the 21st century, a new society is emerging where instead of capital and labour, knowledge is the primary production resource. Efficient utilisation of this existing knowledge can create comprehensive wealth of the nation and also improve the quality of life—in the form of better health, education, infrastructure and other social indicators. Ability to create and maintain the knowledge infrastructure, develop knowledge workers and enhance their productivity through creation, growth and exploitation of new knowledge will be the key factors in deciding the prosperity of this knowledge society. Whether a nation has arrived at the stage of knowledge society is judged by the way the country effectively deals with knowledge creation and knowledge deployment.

Change in employment pattern

In 1960, agriculture sector employed in parts or in full 74% of people of the country and this figure reduced to 62% in 1992 and is expected to further fall to 50% of people in agriculture sector. On the other hand, the demand of agricultural products will double, so an increase in productivity using technology and post-harvest management will have to compensate the manpower reduction in farming and agricultural products sector. In the case of industry, in 1960, 11% of the population was employed in small-scale and large-scale industries. The trend continued with 11% even during 1992. However, it has to increase by 25% in coming decade, as the GDP grows. With high technology, the pattern of employment will take a new shape. Service with knowledge industry component from 15% employability in 1960 has increased to 27% in 1992. And it will further increase to 50% in view of infrastructure maintenance areas, financial sector, IT sector and entertainment industry's demands. This big change will demand more trained skilled human power and technology personnel. Our industrialists, commercial chiefs and technologists may have to get ready for such transformation in agriculture, industries, and service-knowledge industries for which human manpower with knowledge and skills has to be evolved in a mission mode. A nation is made great by the thoughts of its people and their action.

Attaining freedom was the first vision for the nation. This vision was realised in 90 years (1857-1947). It would have been a dream of an individual or collective dream of groups. That dream transformed into thoughts, which lead to revolutionary actions and finally resulted in freedom. In addition, that period of independence movement created great leaders with great actions. Self-reliance in a knowledge society can be the vision for our country today.

Developed India

A nation is made great by the thoughts of its people and their actions. The people in turn become important citizens of that great country. Up to year 2020, I consider, would be a period of technology transformation in India. I anticipate new emerging economic situations. There is a possibility of India becoming a knowledge society with the focused tools of Information Technology and entrepreneurial push. With all these changes, there will be a still greater challenge of keeping our cultural and traditional value system embedded in the Indian minds.

- Knowledge is always the prime mover of prosperity and power.

- The ability to create and maintain the knowledge infrastructure, develop knowledge workers.

- For knowledge industries human knowledge manpower should be created with a mission mode.

- Our culture should be embedded in the minds of this manpower.

FUTURE PERSPECTIVE

21

Don't be afraid to be small

SMALL ENTERPRISES ALSO CONTRIBUTE substantially in the economy of a country. It is thought that in the United States of America, a large percentage of the wealth is generated by the small enterprises that employ less than 50 persons in their establishments. THEY ENCOURAGE SUCH INSTITUTIONS TO GROW.

After independence, the Kirloskar group was the first to offer services to the Railways and the Defence establishments. In order to keep product prices low, Mr. Kirloskar established a network of many small industrial vendors. He helped these small entrepreneurs technically, financially and through training. This was, in fact, the birth of the Small Scale Industry in India. This model may have certain advantages. We need entrepreneurial training, for small enterprises to get established and grow.

Contribution of small entrepreneurs

At present, we are facing a situation in which a large number of youths after completion of senior secondary, graduation, post-graduation and from higher educational institutions are looking for mostly government jobs. Empowering the youth to become wealth creators and job providers instead of being job seekers is the real need of the hour. Recently, attention has been paid to the subject of entrepreneurship, stemming from the experiences from many countries by economic analysts that small firms contribute considerably to economic growth and vitality. Moreover, many people have chosen entrepreneurial careers because doing so seems to offer greater economic and psychological rewards than does the large company route. Recent experiences indicate that the economic progress of few countries, particularly the developed countries, is due to the contribution of a large number of small entrepreneurs employing less than 50 persons in their establishments. We need such entrepreneurs in large numbers in our country for developing and transforming our village clusters into sustainable economic units.

Training for Entrepreneurial leadership

The educational system should equip the students with entrepreneurial leadership. The entrepreneurial leadership has three parts to it.

First, problem finding and problem solving in the context of development. Entrepreneurship starts with understanding our needs and realizing that as human beings we all have similar needs. It begins with wanting to help others as we help ourselves.

In second part, the willingness to take risks. Entrepreneurship requires doing things differently, being bold in our thinking and this is always risky. You must learn how to take calculated risks for the sake of larger gain.

The third part is the disposition to do things right. The school curriculum may be changed in such a way that entrepreneurship is taught.

Development of Entrepreneurs

The key characteristics required in an entrepreneur are DESIRE, DRIVE, DISCIPLINE and DETERMINATION. Following traits are important among the would be entrepreneurs:

a. Vision and pioneering spirit

b. Being able to see possibilities where others do not

c. Always searching for new opportunities and challenges

d. Being creative—'able to think out of the box'

e. Constantly striving to do things better

f. Confident about taking risks

g. Proactive and focused on the future

h. A good knowledge and skill base

Total Quality Management

I have participated in many space and defence programmes. Putting a satellite in the orbit needs a large rocket system. The rocket system and the satellite put together will have at least 50 sub-systems and more than 80 thousand components—mechanical, electrical and chemical. To put a satellite in the orbit, all the systems have to work to full performance requirements. Even if one sub-system or one component fails the total mission will be a failure. Same is true with launching of missile systems. It has to reach the required target by flying thousands of kilometers. The message I would like to convey here is that those in the programme have to learn that the quality of a product has to be built in during the design phase and must be carried forward till the test phase. It has to be constantly improved. The man who designs and manufacturers must love what he does. Entrepreneurs have to aim for total quality management from design to production, testing and marketing. Only this will ensure success of the product and system. This should be taught to the future entrepreneurs with real-life experiences to ensure their success.

TQM and Entrepreneurial Experience

Align the organizational management system, human resource management system and the total quality management system for promoting a successful TQM initiative by any enterprise

Tirupur a case study

Tirupur Knitwear industry is an example of entrepreneurship. The knitwear industry of Tirupur is determined to attain an export target of Rs.1,00,000 crores by 2020. With its unrelenting efforts, Tirupur which has already carved a niche for itself in the knitwear market would soon acquire the image of a prestigious and mature International Knitwear Centre. I am told that almost every household in the town undertakes some activity directly linked to the knitwear industry. The traditional institution of "thottams" has shown its resilience in adapting itself to the new organizational framework of hosiery units. The knitwear industry has been working smoothly through a web of small residence-operated factories to mid-size units, which undertake the task of spinning cotton into yarns, knitting yarn into a fabric, processing and stitching of fabric besides performing contracting and sourcing arrangements. A whole range of industrial units catering to ancillary functions such as manufacture of packing material, stitching material, buttons, zips, tapes have burgeoned thereby providing employment to more than three lac persons.

Productive Employment

The concept of Developed India by 2020, or what is popularly called Vision 2020 means that all Indian people should be prosperous by the year 2020. For wealth to be available to every Indian the key element is productive work, rather productive employment. I emphasise the word productive. TO BE PRODUCTIVE, ONE SHOULD BE ABLE TO ADD VALUE THROUGH SKILLS, OR INTELLECTUAL ACTIVITY OR MANUAL LABOUR OR A COMBINATION.

This value addition will fetch wealth only when the market that is the consumers are satisfied with the added value and there overall satisfaction derived from the goods or services rendered.

It is necessary to impart such skills and knowledge especially to those who are in the lower economic strata of the society. This cannot be done by mere education in letters or numbers. It requires entrepreneurship to spot good economic opportunities, and to have a vision to seize new opportunities.

Vision of an entrepreneur

It is the vision of an entrepreneur which creates new demands for technology, design, management, business and newer levels of productivity and skills. Thus entrepreneurship is an important engine for economic growth. Visionary entrepreneurs, though they may start on a very small scale, create a new world of opportunities. They draw people, even unskilled persons, and transform them into a great human resource, not only for the local market, but also for the global market. The whole area in and around Coimbatore, particularly Tirupur, is blessed with a large number of visionary entrepreneurs in various fields ranging from agriculture, agro processing, herbal products, manufacturing for various sectors' new technologies, education, healthcare, traditional systems of Medicare, and various service industries.

Tirupur is one of the crown jewels in this process of entrepreneurship. The knitwear revolution by the enterprises in Tirupur has been a pride of place in the country. The fact that this economic and entrepreneurial revolution has been achieved without dependence on the government, shows that our people have lots of talent, and that THEY CAN REACH GREAT HEIGHTS IF THEY HAVE A DREAM, HAVE WILL POWER, AND THEY DECIDE TO ACT.

Business persons should co-operate to solve the civic problems such as shortage of energy or waste water recycling along with and in spite of their competition with one another. In Tirupur business persons have got together to themselves solve the shortage of electricity as a co-operative venture. The plans are also being initiated to recycle the waste water.

Another major socio-economic revolution of Tirupur is to draw women on a large scale in the value adding jobs. This has a great significance for the country's development. An economically empowered woman can empower her family and can give her children good education, skills and values.

Let us now look at the future. The global forces, WTO, media—all are in action continuously. Media will show new styles—consumer preferences will change. Other countries will come to poach in your market in India and abroad.

So what is the solution? CONTINUOUSLY INNOVATE. TRY TO THINK BEYOND THE USUAL BEATEN PATHS. For example, the country is rich in traditional design whether it is the Kuravas or Thodas of Tamil or different parts of south or say Rajasthan or North East—where there are wonderful colours and wonderful designs residing in the very homes of weavers. If we apply them in the traditional ways, the productivity will be poor. Use of modern IT and textile engineering techniques, for example, new chemical methods of surface finish etc., can increase the salebility of the products.

- Visionary entrepreneurs, even if they start on a small scale, can create a variety of new opportunities.

- An entrepreneur needs to first discover the gap or need in the market, secondly he/she should be willing to take risk and thirdly should have the capacity and skills to do things right and think out of the box.

- An entrepreneur needs to continuously innovate to secure his/her future and sustain.

22

Think different

I WOULD LIKE TO NARRATE AN EVENT THAT TOOK place in the Rashtrapati Bhavan some years back when I met Bill Gates, the CEO of Microsoft. While taking a walk in the Mughal garden, we were discussing the future challenges in Information Technology, including the issues related to software security. I made a point that we look for open source codes so that we can easily introduce the user built security algorithms. Our discussions became difficult since our views were different. The most unfortunate thing is that India still seems to believe in proprietary solutions. The further spread of IT which is influencing the daily life of individuals would have a devastating effect on the lives of society due to any small shift in the business practice involving these proprietary solutions. It is precisely for these reasons that an open-source software needs to be built, which would be cost-effective for the entire society. In India, the open source code software will have to come and stay in a big way for the benefit of our billion people. IT has to play a major role in this national mission.

Value Addition

Technology and value addition are of prime importance for prosperity of a nation. Value addition in a product per employee today in India is far behind in comparison with other countries such as Thailand, Malaysia, Philippines and Korea. We have to work hard in Value addition techniques in our manufacturing industries, service industry and agriculture sectors. Skilled manpower and capital equipment also need up gradation. Sometime back I came to know that India exports 30 million tonnes of iron ore every year from four of its ports. We should remember that iron ore is not a renewable resource. The steel industry needed is the Industry with the imagination of its people and skills. With the addition of new innovative technologies and the unique management style it should increase the iron content percentage of our ore with appropriate technologies, convert them as steel products, and also design and produce globally competitive new alloy steels. This is the need of the hour. A movement, a methodology for value addition has to be given thrust since it is the main component of the second vision for the nation— Developed India.

Prosperous, happy and peaceful India

A nation's strength predominantly resides in its natural and human resources. As regards natural resources, India is endowed with a vast coastline with marine resources and also oil wealth. In minerals, apart from the conventional material resources, India has the largest deposits of titanium, beryllium and tungsten. India ranks among the top few nations having a rich bio-diversity. Knowledge-based value addition for these natural resources would mean exporting value-added products rather than merely the raw materials. The use of IT for commercialisation and marketing can increase our reach and speed enormously. Our ancient knowledge is a unique resource of India. It has the treasure of a minimum of 5000 years of civilisation. It is essential to leverage this wealth for national well-being as well as to seek a global presence for the nation. A civilisation that does not have the knowledge of technology or the technological nations without experience of civilization cannot innovate newer economy. Human resources, particularly with a large young population, are unique core strength of the nation. This resource can be transformed through various educational and training programmes. Skilled, unskilled and creative manpower can be transformed into wealth generators, particularly in the service sectors and, agro industries. Knowledge-intensive industries can be generated out of our existing industries by injecting demand for high-level software/hardware, which would bring tremendous value addition. It is said, "the precious asset for a company or a country is the skill, ingenuity and imagination of its people." With globalisation, this will become more important because everybody will have access to world class technology and the key distinguishing feature will be the ability of people in different countries to use their imagination to make the best use of the technology." Indeed, development and innovative use of multiple technologies with mission projects and transparent management structure will catapult India into a 'developed nation'.

Inspiring the great mission

What do we need to build developed India? We have resources and we have human power. There are 700 million people below 35 years in the population of a billion people. The nation needs young leaders who can command the transformation of India into a developed nation embedded with knowledge society in the next twenty years.

- Technology and Value addition is one of the prime movers of a country's economy.

- A precious asset for a company and country is the skill and ingenuity of its people and above all innovation.

India of my dreams

The profile of Developed India
before the year 2020

Developed India is a Nation where the rural and urban divide has reduced to a thin line. A Nation where there is an equitable distribution of energy and quality water. A Nation where agriculture, industry and service sector work together in symphony, absorbing technology thereby resulting in sustained wealth generation leading to higher employment potential. A Nation where education is not denied to any meritorious candidate because of the societal or economic conditions. A Nation which is the best destination for the most talented scholars and scientists all over the world.

A Nation where the best of health care is available to all the billion population and the communicable diseases like AIDS/TB, water and vector borne diseases, Cardiac diseases and Cancer are extinct. A Nation where the governance uses the best of the technologies to be responsive, transparent, easily accessible and simple in rules, thereby corruption free. A Nation where poverty has been totally alleviated, where illiteracy and crime against women are eradicated and where the society is unalienated. A Nation that is prosperous, healthy, secure, peaceful and happy. A Nation that is one of the best places to live in, on the earth and brings smiles on billion-plus faces.

23

Unleash the unique software of human genome

I AM RECALLING AN INSPIRING CALL that was the sweat salt of my life:

"WHEN YOU ARE INSPIRED BY SOME GREAT PURPOSE, SOME EXTRAORDINARY PROJECT, ALL YOUR THOUGHTS BREAK THEIR BOUNDS: YOUR MIND TRANSCENDS LIMITATIONS, YOUR CONSCIOUSNESS EXPANDS IN EVERY DIRECTION, AND YOU FIND YOURSELF IN A NEW, GREAT, AND WONDERFUL WORLD. DORMANT FORCES, FACULTIES, AND TALENTS BECOME ALIVE, AND YOU DISCOVER YOURSELF TO BE A GREATER PERSON BY FAR THAN YOU EVER DREAMED YOURSELF TO BE".

Can you think of who would have said this? **It is Maha Rishi Patanjali's 34th Yoga Sutras.** Let this saintly saying enter into our minds and transform the youth of India to sweat for creating a

150

'developed India' in two decades. Fortunately, creativity, imagination and dreaming will always keep the human race supreme. The human genome is full of software that is yet to be activated to unleash the ingenious potentials of the human species. **You have the key.** Harnessing the hidden potential of a soldier will be a winning factor in the future battle.

Nothing is impossible

Here, I would like to narrate an event which took place thirty years ago. In 1976, I was busy with the SLV-3 project in VSSC. For realizing the Inertial Measuring Unit (IMU), we needed a precision IMU housing unit which could house three accelerometers and three rate integrating Gyros and the connected processing electronics. The weight budget given for the entire inertial measuring unit was only three kilogram. Such a precision housing within this weight budget can be made only by using magnesium alloy. I was in search of a foundry which could do this casting since it was a crucial item for the SLV-3 flight. I visited a number of industries, both in the private and public sector. When I asked them, if they could cast the precision IMU housing, all of them told that it would take a minimum of three months for realizing the casting, since they would have to make a metallic mould. In a periodic review of the SLV3 programme by Prof. Satish Dhawan, IMU housing was on the critical path. Then he suggested that a tall scientist working in DMRL, who also was a metallurgist, could help me if I would go and tell him our problem. When I reached DMRL, I found a tall scientist who was busy discussing with his team in one of the laboratories. He was none other than Dr. Arunachalam. He asked me what my problem was. I told him that I needed a magnesium alloy precision casing for the inertial measuring unit within a weight budget of three kilogram. I also told him, I would like to have one unit of the cast casing for testing within a week.

He immediately replied that there would be no problem and that he will get it within a week. He called his team members and explained the task.

The members studied various options. Dr. Arunachalam suggested that they could cast using a thermo-cole mould with certain lining, which is the fastest method to get the casting in time. With this method, I got my magnesium casting within a week. When others were thinking of making regular casting through a metallic die, which is a time-consuming process, Dr. Arunachalam gave me an innovative solution instantaneously to meet the time frame. The only problem here was, that he had to make a mould for every casting. This was my first meeting with Dr. Arunachalam. At that time, I was not aware that I was going to work with him in the DRDO later, nearly for 10 years.

Later, during 1982, Dr. V. S. Arunachalam and Dr. Raja Ramanna were responsible for my re-entry into DRDO from ISRO. Dr. Arunachalam talked to the then Defence Minister, Shri R. Venkatraman, who requested Prof. Satish Dhawan to relieve me from ISRO for taking up the directorship of DRDL.

The period 1982-1992 was an important decade for the DRDO. During this period three major programmes were sanctioned due to the leadership of Dr. V. S. Arunachalam. One was the Integrated Guided Missile Development Programme (IGMDP), second was the light combat aircraft and the third was ATV programme. This was the first time the DRDO budget was increased from two percent of the defence budget to four percent of the defence budget. This was the time innovation in management was also brought in the DRDO. A Board of Management structure was created for IGMDP, a society structure was created for LCA and a hybrid structure was created for ATV. DRDO graduated in this period from an import-substitution establishment to a full-fledged system design and development organization. The strength of the scientists of DRDO also grew to six thousand. Dr. Arunachalam was responsible for injecting these innovations in DRDO. When others were thinking of small projects, Dr. Arunachalam thought of big programmes for the DRDO. When I think of this action, I am reminded of a Thirukkural by the Poet Saint Thiruvalluvar written 2200 years ago. It means that whatever may be the depth of the river or lake or pond, whatever may be the condition of the water, the lily flower always comes out of the water and blossoms. Similarly, if there is a definite determination to achieve a goal even if it looks impossible to achieve, the man succeeds. I find this important characteristic as visualized by Thiruvalluvar is embedded in Dr. Arunachalam.

Visionary zeal

Many programmes which he envisioned in the eighties have now fructified into full-fledged systems. The visionary action taken by Dr. Arunachalam has resulted in two of the strategic missile systems being led into production. The Armed Forces have deployed the systems.

Similarly, I can proudly say that our scientists have designed, developed, tested, evaluated, and integrated the LCA which has logged more than 400 trouble-free flight sorties in three different aircraft.

This is a demonstration of the farsightedness of Dr. Arunachalam in visualizing and getting a complex programme sanctioned for the nation. I have narrated these examples to illustrate how Dr. Arunachalam could create a vision, select the teams and fully empower the scientists to accomplish complex missions so that the country could achieve self-reliance in critical defence systems.

New initiative Kalam-NSS Energy—Space based solar power.

On the 30th May 2010, I addressed the International Space Development Conference (ISDC) where I talked about the possibilities of harvesting energy from space through space based solar power. This conference was attended by many of the experts from the space community, who got interested with the presentation I had made. This led to further discussions and formulations which culminated into the evolution of the idea of Kalam-NSS Energy Initiative with the focus on convergence of competencies from different nations towards the realization of a futuristic mission for green energy from space. On the 4th of November 2010, this initiative was declared to the global audience by National Space Society of United States and was participated by representatives from Indian Space Research Organization and Artemis Innovation Management. Sequence of actions will flow on Kalam-NSS energy in the course of time.

- A great purpose breaks all the rock walls of human limitations and infuses one with a super human energy.
- Those who have a purpose and goal, they find a way. Nothing is impossible for them.

Question: How can we control our mind?

Answer: By fixing a higher goal with indomitable spirit to achieve something beyond us will enable to control our minds and contribute towards a larger cause. Societal missions of bringing happiness to the helpless also enable us to control our minds. Continuous work and right type of thinking is a means of controlling minds. Also failure and problems should not derail a person. WE SHOULD DEFEAT THE PROBLEM INSTEAD OF PROBLEM DEFEATING US.

24
Supremacy of the Human mind

Looking into the Future

RAY KURZWEIL HAS WRITTEN SOME PREDICTIONS in his book "*When Computers Exceed Human Intelligence—The Age of Spiritual Machines*", regarding supremacy of the human mind. According to him World Wide Web will make tremendous impact in the way we communicate and live. Most of the computers and accessories will be micro-sized, wearable and will have wireless communications with each other. Moderately priced PCs capable of performing about billion calculations per second today will be able to perform about trillion calculations per second within next 10 years.

And by 2020 computational ability of an ordinary PC will exceed the capability of human brain. By 2030, the capability of a normal PC would be around 1000 times of human capability.

By the end of this century there would be a strong trend towards merger of human thinking with the world of machine intelligence that the human species initially created. When there would no longer be any clear distinction between human and computers, how are we going to retain the supremacy of man over machines? Computers are going to give us a challenge. It is not only for the biologists and bio-technologists; the entire scientific community would have greater responsibility of keeping the mankind above the man-made computers. Fortunately, the creativity and imagination components of human beings are supreme, and will continue to excel which need to be explored and utilized. The human genome is full of software that is yet to be activated to unleash the ingenious potentials of human species.

Our Challenges in the Planet Earth

There are many challenges for us on our planet earth of six billion people. There is a shortage of water, increased atmospheric pollution leading to many diseases, depleting fossil materials and other natural resources, depletion of available land for agriculture and lack of availability of uniform opportunity to all citizens. Many nations are experiencing the problems of injected terrorism. The young people of the planet are dreaming to live in the land of opportunities and happiness. We have also seen that the economic prosperity of few nations alone has not brought lasting peace to the world. In future, no single nation will be able to handle the situation by itself. Humanity will require mega missions for harnessing solar energy, drinking water from sea water through desalination process and bringing minerals from other planets and also to bring space manufactured products. In such a situation, the present reasons for conflict between nation to nation will become insignificant and unwarranted. India can play a major role in developing a new model of the enlightened citizens centric society which will provide prosperity, peace and happiness to all the nations in the world. **Let me discuss the model:**

Every one of us has gone through the various phases of education from childhood to profession. A scene appears in front of me. When the child is empowered by the parents, at various phases of growth, the child transforms into a responsible citizen. When the teacher is empowered with knowledge and experience, good young human beings with value systems take shape. When an individual or a team is empowered with technology, transformation to higher potential for achievement is assured. When the leader of any institution empowers his or her people, leaders are born who can change the nation in multiple areas. When the women are empowered, society with stability gets assured. WHEN THE POLITICAL LEADERS OF THE NATION EMPOWER THE PEOPLE THROUGH VISIONARY POLICIES, THE PROSPERITY OF THE NATION IS CERTAIN. THE MEDIUM FOR TRANSFORMATION TO DEVELOPED INDIA IS THE EMPOWERMENT AT VARIOUS LEVELS WITH POWER OF KNOWLEDGE OF THE ENLIGHTENED CITIZENS.

Enlightened citizens centric society

As you all know, the United Nations was established in 1945 after the Second World War with the mission of bringing peace among nations and resolving conflicts as they arise so that war will not be waged between nation to nation. The world has witnessed two major unilateral wars in spite of the United Nations.

Hence, we need a world body which can facilitate bringing peace, prosperity and knowledge to the nations, irrespective of the economic status of a particular nation. Indeed, the vision of the **new world**

body has to be for facilitating the evolution of the enlightened citizens in the planet. The Nations will target development milestones in a dynamic environment instead of spending tremendous energy and time in problems initiated by small aims. I visualise, by 2030, the new world body, has to be in its place in the order of global vision - regional co-operation National mission. This is the paradigm shift.

- In the coming times no single nation will be able to resolve all its problems alone.
- We will need mega missions for harnessing world resources and using resources from other planets.
- India should prepare itself for participating in these mega missions.

158

25

Preparing for a Knowledge Society

KNOWLEDGE SOCIETY AND EDUCATION

DURING THE LAST CENTURY, THE WORLD HAS undergone a change from agricultural society, where natural labour was the critical factor, to industrial society where the management of technology, capital and labour provided the competitive advantage. In the 21st century, a new society is emerging where knowledge is the primary resource instead of capital and labour. Such a knowledge society has two important components driven by societal transformation and wealth generation. The societal transformation is on education, healthcare, agriculture and governance. These will lead to employment generation, high productivity and rural prosperity. The wealth generation is an important task for the nation, which has to be woven around national competencies. Core areas have been identified, which will spearhead our movement towards knowledge society.

159

The areas are: Information Technology, bio-technology, weather forecasting, disaster management, tele-medicine and tele-education, technologies to produce native knowledge products, service sector and Infotainment. The driving force for a knowledge society is the primary, secondary and tertiary education.

In the knowledge society, the type of work is less structured and more software driven compared to the industrial economy where the work is structured and hardware driven. For handling this, we need knowledge-based personnel. The worker has to be flexibly skilled and knowledgeable and self empowered. Education system for creating knowledge system worker needs creative, interactive, self-learning and informal environment with the focus on values, merit and quality. The current technology development and open market economy provide more challenge for every citizen in this developing country. If we have to meet the challenge, we need to augment our educational system with innovations such as distance education to meet the aspirations of the large population. Apart from the mission of providing post graduate education, distance education has to promote wide-spread literacy, provide skills to the unskilled and enhance craftsmanship work for realizing large value addition in the rural sector.

Necessary ingredients for Knowledge Society

Knowledge is converted into wealth for social good through the process of innovation. Innovation is an important factor for the competitiveness of both service and manufacturing sectors. Innovation is mainly fed by the dynamic organizational change and also in various walks of life borne out of experiences of individuals and groups and at times from R & D labs as well. Hence, there is an urgent need to establish an efficient innovation system in the country. Such a system would involve the creation of clusters, which are networks of:

a. Inter-dependent firms,

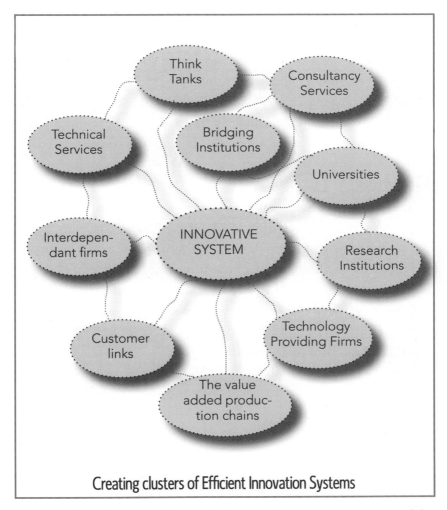

Creating clusters of Efficient Innovation Systems

b. Technology and knowledge producing institutions like universities, colleges and institutes, research institutes, and technology providing firms,

c. Bridging institutions like think tanks, providers of technical or consultancy services, and;

d. Customers' links the value-added production chain

The concept of clusters goes beyond that of a firm network,

as it captures all forms of knowledge sharing and exchange. Thus, an innovative system with its clusters would tap into the growing stock of global knowledge, assimilate and adopt it to local needs and finally create new knowledge and technology. The innovators can replicate their innovations in different parts of the country. Time is now ripe especially since the Government is focused to provide a new deal for the rural India.

The Direction of Innovations

There is always a tendency, even among social institutions and social organisations, including religious institutions that they would like to select well developed parts of states (with few exceptions), and preferably urban areas, for education, healthcare and other socially relevant activities. The innovators should select difficult areas and trigger development to ensure the balanced development of the whole nation. Here I am reminded of an e-mail which I received from one of our citizens. The e-mail reads as follows:

Here is a piece to remind us the importance of sharing of whatever health, wealth or light we have, with the less privileged ones. In an olympiad of mentally handicapped children, in one race, nine contestants, all physically or mentally disabled, assembled at the starting line for the 100 metre race. At the starting signal, they all started out, not exactly in a dash, but with a relish to run the race to the finish and win. One little boy stumbled on the asphalt, tumbled over a couple of times, and began to cry. The other eight heard the boy cry.

They slowed down and looked back. Then they all turned around and went back....every one of them. One girl with Down's syndrome bent down and kissed him and said, "This will make it better." Then all nine linked arms and walked together to the finish line. Everyone in the stadium stood, and the cheering went on for several minutes.

People who were there are still telling the story. Why? Because, deep down, we know this one thing: WHAT MATTERS IN THIS LIFE IS MORE THAN WINNING FOR OURSELVES HELPING OTHERS WIN, EVEN IF IT MEANS SLOWING DOWN AND CHANGING OUR COURSE. I would say that, you do not have to slow down. Rather by helping difficult areas, the feed back will make you go faster. If you pass this on, we may be able to change our hearts as well as someone else's. "A candle loses nothing by lighting another candle".

A noble act will promote creativity and socially conscious society among our billion people and they will all become partners in national development.

- For Global development we need clusters of innovation systems.
- The workers of knowledge society need to be flexibly skilled and knowledgeable and self empowered.
- What matters in this life is to help others to succeed.

26

Dimensions of Spiritual Science

I WOULD LIKE TO SHARE THREE INCIDENTS, which have influenced me. First, one is learning from the life of Imam Ghazali—the indomitable spirit and don't give way to flattery, which influenced me from young age. Second is, my meeting with a 103 years-old sage, radiating the message, "by giving, happiness blossoms" and the third incident is about the message of "nuclear weapon-free world."

Human Indomitable spirit has a blessing of Almighty

Imam Ghazali was a Saint teacher who lived in the 12th Century. When I was young, my father narrated me a scene when Imam Ghazali was tested by *Shaitan*, the transgressed Angel. One day, Imam Ghazali was unfolding his prayer mat for Maharif Namaz. At that time, the *Shaitan* appeared in front of him and said, "Respected Imam Sahib, I am just now coming from heaven where there was a discussion about great human beings, and you have been judged as the best human being living on Earth. As a recognition of your great stature you have been exempted from the trouble of performing Namaz in future. Imam Ghazali was restless as the Namaz time was approaching. So he looked at Shaitan and said, "*Shaitan* Sahib, first of all, performing Namaz is not a trouble at all and when even Prophet Mohammed (peace be upon him), was not exempted from performing Namaz five times a day, how can a poor Imam like me be exempted? Thank you." He went on to perform the Namaz. When he completed the Namaz, Imam Ghazali saw *Shaitan* was still standing. Imam Sahib asked him what he was waiting for. *Shaitan* said, "O Imam you have excelled even the most favoured Prophet Adam, who could not win over my deception, and I made him to eat the forbidden fruit." Realizing that *Shaitan* was flattering, Imam Sahib prayed to Allah, "Oh almighty, help me and save me from the deception of the flattery." Disappointed and failed in his mission *Shaitan* finally disappeared. His mission failed.

The message we derive from the story of Imam Ghazali is that, SPIRITUALITY AND RELIGION SHOULD CREATE AND NURTURE AN INDOMITABLE SPIRIT WHICH CAN RESIST ALL TEMPTATIONS AND CORRUPTION.

Traits of a good human being

I participated in the 102nd birthday celebrations of HH Dr. Sree Sree Sivakumara Mahaswamigalu at Siddaganga Math, Tumkur. His Holiness Sree Sree Sivakumara Swamiji is an example of spreading the message of "giving." He has been on a tireless mission of socio-economic development and eradication of evils of illiteracy and discrimination through giving. He saw education and alleviation of hunger among the masses as an effective means to enrich the human capacity which in turn would contribute to national reconstruction. His Holiness Swamiji has followed the footprints of his Guru of providing free boarding home to the students which is now serving the needs of over 8,000 students. In addition, 2000 pilgrims and visitors in the Math are also provided food every day. During the last seven decades, Swamiji has been the founder of well over 125 educational institutions ranging from nursery to institutions of technology, pure science, arts, management, vocational training and performing arts.

At the end of his birthday function, Mahaswamigal gave an extempore speech for 15 minutes. Based on his century of experience, he said, for developing a happy and peaceful society, each citizen of the nation has to be facilitated to develop two unique traits. ONE IS INTELLECT, AND THE OTHER IS HUMANENESS. THIS CAN BE ACQUIRED THROUGH GOOD PARENTAGE, GOOD TEACHERS, GOOD BOOKS AND BEING IN THE COMPANY OF GREAT PEOPLE. If this is not done at the right age, a human being can become a devil particularly if the intellect acts without humaneness. We as a nation, have to take this message and develop our youth with these traits. The message we derive from the life of HH Dr. Sree Sree Sivakumara Mahaswamigalu is, by giving happiness blossoms in self, others and the world. I composed a poem to celebrate the event, part of the poem is:

Radiating message from Sree Siddaganga Math

You have everything to give.
If you have knowledge, share it.
If you have resources, share it with the needy.
Use your mind and heart,
To remove the pain of the suffering,
And cheer the sad hearts.
In giving, you receive happiness.
Almighty will bless all your actions.

Nuclear weapon-free world is the mission of life

Now I would like to recall the time I spent with a revered Saint who is an epitome of peace. My first experience with Acharya Mahapragya was at Adhyatma Sadhna Kendra, at around midnight at Mehrauli in Oct 1999. On that night, he prayed three times with his distinguished Jain monks for the welfare of the nation and the people. After the prayers, he gave a divine message to me, which still reverberates in my mind. He said, "Kalam, God bless you for what you have done with your team. God Almighty has a bigger mission for you and that is why you are here with me today. I know our country is a nuclear nation now. The mission for you is greater than what you and your team have done, and it is greater than any human being had ever done. The nuclear weapons are proliferating in tens and thousands in the world. I command you and you only with all the divine blessings at my disposal to invent a 'peace system' and find a solution to make the same nuclear weapons ineffective, insignificant and politically inconsequential." When Acharyaji finished his great advice, there was a pin drop silence. It appeared to me as though the confluence of heavens concurred with the saintly message. This command shook me for the first time in my 68 years of life (I was 68 at that time). It has since then become a challenge working on me and has become a motto of my life.

Divine Science

Scientists, philosophers and theologists and Spiritual leaders have to eventually converge towards an understanding, what may be called divine science. The world is looking for a new science; that must be Divine Science. These are spiritual, mystical, religious and theological truths of the contemporary world. The Divine Science would be a result of breakthroughs in understanding the fundamental basis of reality such as quantum theory, relativity theory, chaos theory, general systems theory, string theory, and others. The magnitude of infinite possibilities within the human body and external cosmos is amazing. THE DIVINE SCIENCE HAS TO TRANSCEND THE CERTAINTY OF A STRICTLY NEWTONIAN CLOCKWORK NOTION TO A NEW VISION OF A HOLISTIC AND UNIFIED COSMOS ROOTED IN A NON-LOCAL QUANTUM REALITY THAT IS FUNDAMENTALLY SPIRITUAL AS OPPOSED TO MATERIAL. It may also be described as intrinsically evolutionary and harmonious.

Now, I would like to discuss about how through a Multipronged action, the evolution of enlightened society can be realized in the global community.

I would like to recall a unique incident which gave me a message of unity of minds. During the year 2003, I visited one of the Indian states, Arunachal Pradesh. I visited a Buddhist monastery at Tawang, at an altitude of 3500 meters. I stayed and spent some time, nearly a day, there. I observed a unique situation in all the villages nearby where young and experienced were all radiating happiness in spite of severe winter conditions. Then, I visited the 400-year-old Tawang monastery where I saw monks of all age groups in a state of serenity. I was asking myself what is the unique feature of Tawang and surrounding villages, that makes people and monks to be at peace with themselves. When the time came, I asked the Chief Monk, how in Tawang villages and monastery, I am experiencing peace and happiness being radiated by everyone. There was a pause, the chief monk smiled. He said, "You are the President of India. You will be knowing all about us and the whole nation." Again, I said, "It is very important for me, you please give me your thoughtful analysis."

There was a beautiful golden image of Lord Buddha radiating smile and peace. The Chief Monk assembled nearby all his nearly 100 young and experienced monks. The Chief Monk and myself were sitting amidst them. The Chief Monk gave a short discourse, which I would like to share with you. Chief Monk said, **"In the present world, we have a problem of distrust, unhappiness transforming into violence. This monastery spreads: when you "Remove "I" and "Me" from your mind, you will eliminate ego; if you get rid of ego, hatred towards fellow human beings will vanish; if the hatred goes out of our mind, the violence in thinking and action will disappear; if violence in our mind is taken away, peace springs in human minds. Then peace and peace and peace alone will blossom in the society."** I realized the meaning of beautiful equation for peaceful life, but difficult mission for the individual is how to remove the ethos, of "I" and "ME." For this, we need the education inculcated in the young age as propagated by the great philosophers. The message we derive out of this experience is the need to rise above ego and negative thoughts, and transform them into positive thoughts of compassion for all humanity. This is the key for a happy, peaceful and prosperous society.

- Human beings should develop two unique traits of. intellect and humaneness

- Giving brings happiness.

- Remove **I** and **Me** from your mind, you will eliminate ego and get peace and happiness.

World Vision 2030

Global world system for prosperity and peace

Evolution of better world is possible only if we evolve a better nation with peace and prosperity. India has a vision to realize peace and prosperity as per the Vision 2020. What should be the World Vision to achieve Global World System for prosperity and peace. Recently I had an opportunity to take a course on "Evolution of Happy, Prosperous and Peaceful Societies" at the Gatton College of Business and Economics at the University of Kentucky, Lexington, USA. Based on the experience with the course participants, I have been discussing with the students from multiple institutions, and disciplines, on ideas which can lead to the realization of a World Vision 2030. Let me present to you these visualizations.

1. A world of nations where people live in a green clean environment without pollution.
2. A world of nations having prosperity without poverty,
3. A world of nations with creative leadership that ensures effective mechanisms to resolve conflicts between nations and societies in a timely manner keeping overall peace and prosperity of the world as a goal.
4. A world of nations having peace without fear of war and a happy place to live for all humankind

This is the kind of the world which we have to bequeath to the youth of the world. The foundation of the world vision 2030 shall be enshrined in regional cooperation and development. The regional development will ultimately empower the individual nations to realise the vision.

Books as companions

I have a message for the young and old,
always have books as companions.
Books were always my friends Since last more
than 50 years books gave me dreams.
Dreams resulted in Missions.
Books helped me to take up the missions confidently.
Good Books for me were angels. They gave me courage,
at the time of failures and touched
my heart gently at the time of success.
Hence, I ask young friends to have books as friends
Books are your great friends.
My home Library is the greatest
Beautiful song and the greatest
Wealth of my life.

Five books, that have made a difference in my life.

THIRUKURAL *by Thiruvalluvar*

EVERYDAY GREATNESS *by Stephen Covey*

FIVE MINDS FOR THE FUTURE *by Howard Gardner*

LIGHT FROM MANY LAMPS *by Lillian Eichler Watson*

EMPIRES OF THE MIND *by Denis Waitley*

Question: If God granted you one wish, what would you ask for?

Answer: I will pray to god to give me strength to work for universal peace and prosperity.

Question: How would you like to be remembered?

Answer: He brought smiles on millions and millions of faces. I will work for it.